**New Directions for
Institutional Research**

Robert K. Toutkoushian
EDITOR-IN-CHIEF

J. Fredericks Volkwein
ASSOCIATE EDITOR

Reframing Persistence Research to Improve Academic Success

Edward P. St. John
Michael Wilkerson
EDITORS

Number 130 • Summer 2006
Jossey-Bass
San Francisco

REFRAMING PERSISTENCE RESEARCH TO IMPROVE ACADEMIC SUCCESS
Edward P. St. John, Michael Wilkerson (eds.)
New Directions for Institutional Research, no. 130
Robert K. Toutkoushian, Editor-in-Chief

NEW DIRECTIONS FOR INSTITUTIONAL RESEARCH (ISSN 0271-0579, electronic ISSN 1536-075X) is part of The Jossey-Bass Higher and Adult Education Series and is published quarterly by Wiley Subscription Services, Inc., A Wiley Company, at Jossey-Bass, 989 Market Street, San Francisco, California 94103-1741 (publication number USPS 098-830). Periodicals Postage Paid at San Francisco, California, and at additional mailing offices. POSTMASTER: Send address changes to New Directions for Institutional Research, Jossey-Bass, 989 Market Street, San Francisco, California 94103-1741.

SUBSCRIPTIONS cost $80.00 for individuals and $170.00 for institutions, agencies, and libraries. See order form at end of book.

EDITORIAL CORRESPONDENCE should be sent to Robert K. Toutkoushian, Educational Leadership and Policy Studies, Education 4220, 201 N. Rose Ave., Indiana University, Bloomington, IN 47405.

New Directions for Institutional Research is indexed in *College Student Personnel Abstracts, Contents Pages in Education,* and *Current Index to Journals in Education* (ERIC).

Microfilm copies of issues and chapters are available in 16mm and 35mm, as well as microfiche in 105mm, through University Microfims, Inc., 300 North Zeeb Road, Ann Arbor, Michigan 48106-1346.

www.josseybass.com

CONTENTS

Editors' Notes

For decades, persistence researchers have considered implications for institutional practice, but there has been little applied research that examines the effects of the remedies recommended by the researchers. Instead, it is widely assumed we know a great deal about "best practices" and that we should organize professional programs for college personnel to promote these practices. However, what if the recommended practices do not work as well as intended? What if recurring challenges go unaddressed even when the best-practices approach is used? If the demographics of student populations change, does conventional wisdom about best practices still apply? And what if, due to revenue constraints, student affairs and academic administrators are forced to redirect their efforts to address these critical challenges?

While standard persistence research is well positioned to continue producing replicated studies for systematic review and comparison, the more difficult issues related to improving academic success for an increasingly diverse student clientele go largely unaddressed. Braxton's *Reworking the Student Departure Puzzle* (2000) introduced variations on the common theoretical lenses used to study diversity, but that volume did not address the more applied challenge of using persistence research to support academic improvement. In comparison to the persistence research tradition as we have known it, we now face a street-level, working-class challenge: to provide high-quality institutional research that not only informs difficult institutional decisions about resource reallocation but that also encourages practitioners—college teachers and student affairs administrators—to face up to the critical challenges now facing higher education. With increasing numbers and diversity of students on the one hand and declining public financial support on the other, many colleges and universities face critical challenges in their efforts to improve student success.

This volume of *New Directions for Institutional Research* takes a step forward in higher education research by introducing a new approach to applied inquiry and evaluation. Rather than engaging in paradigmatic persistence research that has vague implications for practice, the authors in this volume begin the process of addressing the more elusive goal of conducting applied studies that can be used to inform faculty and administrators about and engage them in the process of changing their institutions by enabling and encouraging them to experiment with new approaches to their most critical challenges.

At this point, some skeptical readers may be harboring doubts about these claims, especially the notion that persistence research has not provided

New Directions for Institutional Research, no. 130, Summer 2006 © Wiley Periodicals, Inc.
Published online in Wiley InterScience (www.interscience.wiley.com) • DOI: 10.1002/ir.175

1

sound evaluative information. As it turns out, this claim has a sound basis and it provides a point of departure for this volume. Three of the chapters in this volume were prepared for a planning project that aimed to develop a new center for persistence research and the support of change. What we learned from these thoughtful pieces was that a new approach was needed. We needed to rethink the role of institutional research in support of academic improvement. Based on this reflection, we decided to take a more action-oriented approach using research to support assessment and an inquiry-based approach to encourage and engage in reform. Three of the chapters in this volume also illustrate how this new approach can work.

Rethinking Persistence Research

The planning project for a new retention center began as an idea that would build on years of work in Indiana and elsewhere that focused on retention. We thought Indiana University would be a good place for such a center, not only because several established persistence scholars were there, but also because there had been a large investment in retention projects by Lilly Endowment and Lumina Foundation for Education. Surely this was the place to start. As a first step in the project, Charlie Nelms, the Principal Investigator for the project (and Indiana University's Vice President for Institutional Development and Student Affairs), asked Don Hossler to review existing persistence research to see what had been learned about the types of programs that improve persistence. The answer was a surprise.

In Chapter One, Lori Patton, Carla Morelon, Dawn Michele Whitehead, and Hossler summarize their review of prior research. Surprisingly, to us at least, there were very few studies of the impact of interventions on persistence, with the exception of a rather large body of research on the effects of financial aid on persistence. The authors reviewed the major journals with research on college students and found only a few examples of rigorous studies supporting only limited conclusions. When these findings were presented to representatives of a number of Indiana's colleges and universities in the spring of 2003, they were received with disbelief. Certainly it was not true in Indiana, they argued, especially since the Lilly Endowment had required evaluations of the effects of their investments. Because it is possible that applied studies are done but not published, we decided to test this claim and solicited every evaluation study that could be found in the state or that campuses were willing to have reviewed.

In addition, we went to one of the nation's persistence experts to review these studies. We wanted to learn that Indiana was indeed different and allowed our bias to show through. In Chapter Two, John M. Braxton, Jeff McKinney, and Pauline J. Reynolds present their review of the Indiana studies. While a number of studies combined documentation of programs with reviews of trends in persistence rates, very few actually provided well-designed evaluations that controlled for other variables that might influence persistence. Using a reasonable quality standard, Braxton and his research assistants found only a few noteworthy examples, but far fewer than we expected.

As part of the planning process, Deborah Faye Carter collaborated with the planning team in the review of prior research. In Chapter Three, Dr. Carter reviews the research on minority-student persistence, one of the critical challenges facing Indiana higher education. Once a challenge is identified, it is important to look externally as well as internally for possible solutions. In this case, Carter reviews the research—a major external source of information—to discern what can be learned from prior research.

Refocusing on Academic Success

Throughout this period of review, we listened to our critics as well, in particular, our colleague in Indianapolis, Victor Borden, who kept reminding us that we "research types" kept overlooking the real-life problems of institutional research professionals who seek better ways to engage in collaborative research with faculty and administrators. In Chapter Four, Michele J. Hansen and Victor M.H. Borden introduce a new way of viewing the persistence problem. They argue that research should be used to support improvement in academic success. Rather than evaluate, researchers should first collaborate on building an understanding of the problem, support and inform the redesign of practice, and assist with the evaluations, using the results to inform practice. While their example used qualitative methods, it also seems possible to use quantitative methods in this type of collaborative process.

The four thoughtful and provocative chapters that form the first half of this volume provided a substantial portion of the new foundations for conceptualizing the Indiana Project on Academic Success (IPAS). Our aims were not only to be more applied than was evidenced in the tradition of persistence research, but also to be supportive of change. I had for years been advocating an inquiry-based approach to reform in higher education (St. John, 1994, 1995; St. John and Paulsen, 2001), a notion that was based on my experience with K-12 school reform (Finnan, St. John, McCarthy, and Slovacek, 1995; St. John, Griffith, and Allen-Haynes, 1997) but that had not been systematically tested in higher education.

Rather than argue for a retention center—and with the encouragement of Lumina Foundation to think differently about the problem—we embarked on a new approach. IPAS introduced a new, inquiry-based approach to reform, as detailed in Table 1. The process starts with assessment—not to prove success but to uncover critical challenges that cry out for attention. In this view, if assessment does not uncover challenges, then it has failed our intent for reform. In the normal course of institutional behavior, critical recurring challenges often go unaddressed—or at least so we thought.

Table 1. Overview of the Stages in the IPAS Process

Stage 1 Assessment	• Compare campus assessment information to statewide assessment results; identify possible challenges. • Collect additional information from campus sources, such as prior reports and studies and focus group interviews. • Organize teams of administrators, faculty, professional staff, and students to identify critical challenges on the campus. • Prioritize the challenges, identifying two or three that merit special attention at a campus level.
Stage 2 Organizing	• Coordinate the assessment and inquiry process with campus-level planning and budgeting; integrate the challenges with strategic plans; coordinate budgeting to provide necessary support. • Appoint workgroups to address critical, campus-wide challenges; consider providing release time to team leaders to work on tasks for the campus. • Coordinate the inquiry process (activities of the workgroups) with campus planning and budgeting.
Stage 3 Action Inquiry	Each campus workgroup engages in a process to 1. Build an Understanding of the Challenge 2. Look Internally and Externally for Solutions 3. Assess Possible Solutions 4. Develop Action Plans 5. Implement Pilot Test and Evaluate
Stage 4 Evaluation	The campus coordinating teams • Coordinate implementation and evaluation, review plans, encourage presentations to campus planning groups, and help coordinate the inquiry process with campus planning. • Coordinate evaluation support of pilot tests with the IPAS project team and campus groups.

Source: The IPAS Resource Guide, 2004, Indiana Project on Academic Success.

The assessment phase of this project involved the following activities:

- Assessing statewide student outcomes using state-level databases and parallel campus-specific assessments
- Introducing the assessment process to participating colleges in a workshop, providing statewide assessment results and campus analyses
- Encouraging campuses to uncover their own critical challenges using our analyses or existing evidence from their own work to identify campus needs

After the campuses completed their assessments, we encouraged them to organize staff workgroups to address the challenges using inquiry, with IPAS staff providing technical support for the workgroups. A team of professionals and graduate students functioned as consultants to the campuses. We think that this process has helped document and illustrate an alternative approach to technical support.

The statewide assessment used a statewide database to examine the 2000 high school cohort's preparation, college-enrollment decisions, and persistence (St. John, Musoba, and Chung, 2004). We found a relationship between high school curricula and SAT scores, college enrollment, and persistence. We also found that student financial aid was linked to these outcomes. However, when we shared the results with the campuses, we learned we needed to examine the pathways of nontraditional students as well, so we engaged in a large number of additional analyses in support of the campuses.

While the statewide research is not the focal point of this volume, one set of results merits note: our analyses of persistence by racial or ethnic groups (St. John, Carter, Chung, and Musoba, 2006). In the persistence analyses for whites and for the population as a whole, we found—controlling for background, preparation, and other factors—that having declared a major was positively associated with persistence during the first two years of college.

As Carter discusses in Chapter Three, the analyses of persistence by African Americans found that students who had declared majors were less likely to persist—controlling for these same variables. Although high-achieving African Americans were more likely to have declared their majors—controlling for prior preparation—they were also more likely to drop out. This issue, along with the need to serve nontraditional-age and working students better, became major statewide challenges.

Two of the chapters in this volume illustrate that university-based inquiry, coupled with technical support from professional staff, can provide campuses with the support needed to engage in research-informed change. Once our participating campuses had gone through their own assessment processes, most identified critical challenges. When issues were large and cut across campuses, we conducted literature reviews to see what we could learn. We also provided technical support for campuses to use inquiry to address their challenges and to evaluate the results of their interventions.

The inquiry process itself involves focusing on possible explanations for the challenges and identifying solutions that merit testing in practice. We encouraged teams on the campuses to identify a range of possible solutions, to assess which ones had the best chances of addressing the challenge, and to test them through practice. In Chapter Five, St. John, McKinney, and Tina Tuttle describe the action-inquiry process and the roles of technical assistance providers and present a couple of campus examples. They also describe how the inquiry process was adapted at a few campuses to integrate evaluation into the process of building understanding of the challenge, closing the loop.

The underlying challenge in the process of change on many college and university campuses is to use evaluation research systematically to examine the effects of intervention. Rather than viewing the aim of evaluation as the validation of decisions, we see it as part of the process of discovering better ways of addressing critical, recurring challenges. In Chapter Six, Glenda Droogsma Musoba provides background on the workable-models approach to evaluation research used in this study and provides an example of an evaluation study. This type of research moves a step closer to meeting the standards set by Patton, Braxton, and their colleagues in the early chapters.

Lessons Learned

This volume introduces an alternative way to think about the role of institutional research in support of institutional improvement and student academic success. Consider the path we are on. Policymakers are introducing new approaches to assessment and finance that reward institutions with high persistence rates (St. John, Kline, and Asker, 2001; Zumeta, 2001). But this systematic approach could turn into a means of rewarding institutions that attract the most able students who can afford to pay the costs of attending. In other words, we need to focus on improving opportunity for new, first-generation college students and others who challenge traditional assumptions about academic success.

To meet the goal of expanding higher education for new generations of first-generation college students, we need to learn about new pathways to success. The concluding chapter summarizes the lessons learned from this initial foray into the use of institutional research to support changes aimed at improving academic success. While the impact of this new venture may be modest, we hope it raises the prospect of change by introducing an alternative approach to technical and research support for reform in higher education.

> Edward P. St. John
> Michael Wilkerson
> Editors

References

Braxton, J. M. (ed.). *Reworking the Student Departure Puzzle.* Nashville, Tenn.: Vanderbilt University Press, 2000.

Finnan, C. R., St. John, E. P., McCarthy, J., and Slovacek, S. P. (eds.). *Accelerated Schools in Action: Lessons from the Field.* Thousand Oaks, Calif.: Corwin Press, 1995.

St. John, E. P. *Prices, Productivity, and Investment: Assessing Financial Strategies in Higher Education.* ASHE-ERIC Higher Education Report, no. 3. Washington, D.C.: George Washington University, 1994.

St. John, E. P. "Rethinking Tuition and Student Aid Strategies." In E. P. St. John (ed.), *Rethinking Tuition and Student Aid Strategies.* New Directions for Higher Education, no. 89. San Francisco: Jossey-Bass, 1995.

St. John, E. P., Carter, D. F., Chung, C. G., and Musoba, G. D. "Diversity and Persistence in Indiana Higher Education: The Impact of Preparation, Major Choices, and Student Aid." In E. P. St. John (ed.), *Readings on Equal Education.* Vol. 21: *Public Policy and Educational Opportunity: School Reforms, Postsecondary Encouragement, and State Policies on Higher Education* (pp. 359–410). New York: AMS Press, 2006.

St. John, E. P., Griffith, A. I., and Allen-Haynes, L. *Families in Schools: A Chorus of Voices in Restructuring*. Portsmouth, N.H.: Heinemann, 1997.

St. John, E. P., Kline, K. A., and Asker, E. H. "The Call for Public Accountability: Rethinking the Linkages to Student Outcomes." In D. E. Heller (ed.), *The States and Public Higher Education: Affordability, Access, and Accountability*. Baltimore: Johns Hopkins University Press, 2001.

St. John, E. P., Musoba, G. D., and Chung, C. G. "Academic Preparation and College Success: Analyses of Indiana's 2000 High School Class." Report prepared for the Indiana Commission on Higher Education and the Lumina Foundation for Education. Bloomington: Indiana Project on Academic Success, 2004.

St. John, E. P., and Paulsen, M. B. "The Finance of Higher Education: Implications for Theory, Research, Policy and Practice." In M. B. Paulsen and J. C. Smart (eds.), *The Finance of Higher Education: Theory, Research, Policy, and Practice*. New York: Agathon, 2001.

Zumeta, W. "Public Policy and Accountability in Higher Education: Lessons from the Past and Present for the New Millennium." In D. E. Heller (ed.), *The States and Public Higher Education Policy: Affordability, Access, and Accountability*. Baltimore: Johns Hopkins University Press, 2001.

EDWARD P. ST. JOHN *is Algo D. Henderson Collegiate Professor of Education at the Center for the Study of Higher and Postsecondary Education at the University of Michigan. His research focuses on educational policy and public finance in both K-12 and higher education.*

MICHAEL WILKERSON *is a professional writer now working as coordinator of university arts initiatives at Indiana University. His interest in retention stems from his involvement with the highly successful, though slightly documented, IU Intensive Freshman Seminars and from his service as the university's coordinator of academic affairs in the office of the vice president for academic affairs from 1997 through 2001.*

NEW DIRECTIONS FOR INSTITUTIONAL RESEARCH • DOI: 10.1002/ir

1

*There has been very little previous evaluation research
that examines the effects of interventions on persistence.*

Campus-Based Retention Initiatives: Does the Emperor Have Clothes?

*Lori D. Patton, Carla Morelon, Dawn Michele Whitehead,
Don Hossler*

In a recent meeting of senior campus administrators, one of the vice presidents commented, "I have set aside $300,000 for retention initiatives to be implemented over the next two years. My question is, on which programs should I spend these dollars?" These kinds of conversations take place on the campuses of colleges and universities each year. Since the mid-1970s, perhaps no other topic in the published literature has garnered the attention of higher education researchers and administrators more than student persistence. Indeed, the field of higher education now sports a journal that is devoted to the topic of student retention. This article describes our attempt to conduct a systematic review and critique of the research that has been done on campus-based retention initiatives.

It is important for us to define clearly the boundaries of our efforts. Hundreds of studies have tested assumptions of theories of student departure. Some examples include the following: Bean (1990), Mallette and Cabrera (1991), Munro (1981), Pascarella, Duby, and Iverson (1983), Pascarella and Terenzini (1983), Stage (1989), Stoeker, Pascarella, and Wolfle (1988), Tinto (1993), and Williamson and Creamer (1989). Efforts to test the models of Tinto (Braxton, Sullivan, and Johnson, 1997; Cabrera, Stampen, and Hansen, 1990; Halpin, 1990; Hurtado and Carter, 1997; Milem and Berger, 1997; Nora, Attinasi, and Matonak, 1990; Tierney, 1992) and Bean (Andreu, 2002; Farabaugh-Dorkins, 1991; Himelhoch, Nichols, Ball, and Black, 1997; Stahl and Pavel, 1992) dominate this line of research. Although these theories and

New Directions for Institutional Research, no. 130, Summer 2006   © Wiley Periodicals, Inc.
Published online in Wiley InterScience (www.interscience.wiley.com) • DOI: 10.1002/ir.176

the efforts to test the properties of each model are useful, they do not provide empirical analyses of campus-based programs that purportedly enhance student persistence. This paper examines the existing published research on college student retention in order to determine the extent to which the assertions about enhancing student persistence have been confirmed through rigorous analysis and program evaluation.

Methodology and Preliminary Results

The first step in this research effort was to examine the assertions made about campus programs and strategies to decrease student dropout rates at universities. Published articles, both empirical and propositional, were reviewed in order to develop a comprehensive list of the assertions made about the efficacy of various retention initiatives. After identifying the assertions, we grouped them into similar categories and began our literature searches in electronic databases and relevant published journals.

We reveal one of our most important findings early in this chapter when we note that this study immediately produced initial findings that in some respects are as interesting as the actual results of our analyses. We say this because one of the most important findings of this investigation is the dearth of evidence to support the claims proffered on the efficacy of a wide range of campus-based retention initiatives.

As a form of quality control, we limited our search to propositional and research-based published studies in first- and second-tier journals that commonly publish research in the field of higher education. Working within these guidelines, we conducted a thorough review of approximately one hundred published research reports on student persistence. In selecting articles for this chapter, each published article was reviewed and evaluated using the following criteria: a detailed description of the programmatic intervention, methodological rigor in the sampling strategies, and analytic rigor of data analytic techniques. Using these criteria we grouped all of the articles into three categories: most rigorous, moderately rigorous, and least rigorous.

The articles we determined to be most rigorous typically included most of the following attributes: they yielded statistically significant results or provided strong qualitative findings, they included large sample sizes, they included some form of a control group, and they contained detailed information about the retention-centered program. Studies deemed to be of moderate rigor usually had a modicum of information about the retention-based program and more simplistic and less robust analytical findings. Articles judged to be of low rigor had important limitations, such as no description of statistical tests used to assess the program's effectiveness, a very small number of students who participated in the study, or little information about the retention program that was implemented.

Our search identified a large set of assertions about campus-based programs and strategies to enhance student persistence; however, too often we could find little or no supporting evidence for the claims often made about strategies to enhance persistence. In other instances, the research did indicate that campus-based interventions were linked to positive changes in student retention.

We found it possible to group the studies we reviewed in several different ways. After considerable review, we aggregated the studies into the following groupings: counseling and mentoring programs (four articles); learning communities, living-learning communities, and structured academic experiences (four articles); student-faculty interaction (three articles), and transition programs (five articles). In the following sections we describe the groupings of studies in each area and then present our findings and summarize our results. In the implications section, we offer suggestions for campus administrators involved in efforts to improve persistence and graduation rates and for researchers conducting evaluation and assessment studies of student retention programs.

Limitations

The most obvious limitation is the fact that administrators of retention programs are most often members of a small team or solo administrators who have neither the time nor the resources to do more than administer their programs. In addition, we did not search papers, for example, given at scholarly conferences or those catalogued in the ERIC system. Rather, we used the quality control embedded in the review process of scholarly journals as one of our primary criteria for the selection of studies to review. Finally, we used restricted criteria in our search for published articles. We looked only for articles that provided a direct link between institutional programming and retention. Undoubtedly, a number of research articles that do not refer directly to programs could possibly shed some light on other factors that contribute to undergraduate student persistence.

Another important limitation is that none of the studies we reviewed employed sophisticated methods to control for biases that could result from self-selection. Increasingly, researchers have been developing statistical techniques to compensate for potential selection-bias problems (Bifulco, 2002; Hoxby, 2002), but research on programmatic efforts to enhance student persistence are just beginning to employ these methods. As a result, there was little we could do to compensate for this limitation at the time this investigation was conducted.

Findings

We found a limited number of assessments of the efficacy of counseling or mentoring interventions. Our literature review identified only four empirical studies that focused on the impact of these kinds of programs.

Counseling Programs. In a study of high rigor, Turner and Berry (2000) examined the impact of counseling center services on retention at a western state university. This study included a comparison group and a large number of students. Over the course of the study, as many as 70 percent of the students who used the counseling center reported that personal problems were affecting their grades; however, only one in five of those who used counseling services indicated considering withdrawal; more than 60 percent said the counseling was helpful in maintaining or improving their academic performance. In addition nearly 44 percent indicated that counseling helped them to persist. The authors found that students who followed up and used the services of the counseling center had annual retention rates of 70.9 percent in comparison to the general student population, which had a retention rate of 58.6 percent ($p < .001$); counseled students also had higher return enrollment rates than noncounseled students (77.2 percent versus 67.9 percent; $p < .001$). On average, counseling clients achieved a total retention rate of 85.2 percent, whereas the general student rate was 73.8 percent.

Wilson, Mason, and Ewing (1997) conducted a study of moderate rigor of the impact of counseling. They found that students who indicated a retention concern and sought counseling had a higher retention rate than students who had previously requested counseling but did not receive it. In an examination of the academic records of 562 students (the demographic makeup of the sample was comparable to the university population), those who received from one to seven counseling sessions were either retained or graduated at a rate of 79 percent, in comparison to noncounseled students, who were retained at a rate of 65 percent. A 2 × 4 chi square table indicated that as the number of counseling sessions increased, the likelihood of retention increased as well.

Mentoring Programs. Johnson (1989) claims that mentoring programs provide students with resources and get them actively involved in their own learning. A number of programs are cited, yet we were unable to find much empirical support for the claim. Jacobi (1991) conducted an extensive review of the mentoring literature and found that studies on mentoring were rare and tended to be methodologically weak. We found two studies of mentoring programs.

Dale and Zych (1996) conducted a study, judged to be of low rigor, of the HORIZONS program, a freshman student support program housed at Purdue University. University staff and HORIZONS alumni serve as mentors for low-income, first-generation, and disabled students. The HORIZONS group was compared to a control group of first-year students; both groups consisted of eight Hispanics, fourteen African Americans, and twenty-five white students. The program consisted of content-oriented instruction focusing on academic skills and strategy development; it is presented in conjunction with process-oriented instruction focusing on developmental and affective skills. Dale and Zych found that the retention rate for the HORIZONS group during the first and second semester was 100 percent, while the control group's retention rate dropped from 100 percent to 89 percent between these semesters. The researchers also found that 85 percent of the HORIZONS group graduated or were working toward graduation, as opposed to the 47 percent of the control group who had either graduated or were working toward graduation. The sample size in this study was small, and only descriptive statistics were provided to support the effectiveness of the program.

The Ethnic Mentor Undergraduate (EMU) program was designed to increase the number of underrepresented ethnic students in the educational pipeline in the College of Health and Human Services at a state university (Thile and Matt, 1995). In order to explore the effectiveness of this program, thirty-two incoming students (seventeen first-year students, fifteen transfer students) participated in the study. The authors of this study compared participants in the EMU program with students who were enrolled but not participants in the program. In addition to being paired with faculty mentors, the first-year students were paired with seniors while junior transfer students were paired with graduate students, matching ethnicity and major as closely as possible. Embracing students' ethnic-cultural background, unique strengths, skills, experiences, and learning styles, the program endeavored to capture and cultivate these attributes during the students' tenure at the institution. Academic and personal-social elements were introduced to students to provide balanced exposure to and enhancement in both areas.

The authors of this high-rigor study examined the mean GPA of the students in the EMU program. The group's mean GPA (2.95) was comparable to the all-university average, and their average SAT score of 755 was well below that average. However, after one year in the program, 82 percent of the EMU first-year students and 87 percent of the junior transfers persisted. The authors reported that the differences among all first-year students and EMU first-year students were not significant. For this study, however, finding similar persistence rates can be viewed as an indicator of the efficacy of the program, since the average SAT score of the participants was lower than that of the rest of the student body. In addition, the differences among transfer students were significant at the .05 level.

In total, these two studies led us to conclude that there is at best weak support for the assertion that mentoring programs are effective vehicles to improve the retention rates of undergraduate students. The few investigations, one of them of low rigor, combined with the results, did not fully establish the efficacy of the interventions and led to the conclusion that the evidence for mentoring programs improving retention rates was not strong.

The cumulative evidence from these studies of the impact of counseling and mentoring provides, at best, moderate support for the efficacy of these programs in enhancing student persistence. First, there are few (four) research-based published studies on this topic. Each of these studies found evidence that counseling and mentoring did have a positive impact on student retention. However, some of the studies provided only minimal details about the statistical analyses that were used to assess the programs, others had small sample sizes, making the generalizability of the findings difficult. The pattern across these studies was moderately supportive of the assertion that counseling and mentoring programs can help to improve student persistence. We found no evidence to support the positive impact of other forms of support, such as career advising.

Learning Communities, Living-Learning Communities, and Structured Academic Experiences. Astin (1985) characterizes a learning community (LC) as a small cluster of students who participate in an environment designed to foster cohesiveness, shared purpose, and an integrated, continuous path of in-class and out-of-class experiences. Schuh (2004) states that "the environment created in a campus residence contributes to student learning by providing opportunities to experience diversity, to be challenged by their peers, and to learn from one another" (p. 284). Living-learning communities are important because, when designed properly, they create a seamless learning environment that integrates both academic and social experiences that contribute to student development.

Attempts to garner the presumed benefits of LCs are not limited to residential institutions. Some community colleges have adopted the idea of creating learning communities for commuter students. Despite the fact that such communities do not have a residential aspect, students are still assigned to smaller groups and placed in the same cluster of classes and exposed to similar opportunities that foster a sense of community and belonging. While learning communities at both four-year institutions and community colleges sound promising, we found very little research to support such assertions about their effectiveness. Overall, we identified five articles that dealt with living-learning communities.

In a highly rigorous investigation, Pascarella and Terenzini (1980a) conducted a study with three purposes: to verify the presumed social-psychological and interpersonal dimensions underlying an experimental living-learning community, to determine the main and interaction effects of an LC on a range of first-year educational outcomes, and to determine the impact of faculty and peer interaction within the LC context. The longitudinal study was conducted among a sample of first-year students at a large, private residential university.

The researchers found that when pre-enrollment characteristics were held constant, exposure to the LC was significantly and positively associated with retention. They also found that the structural arrangements of the LC facilitated informal interactions with faculty, and that the quality of those interactions probably accounted for the differences between the residents' and nonparticipants' levels of satisfaction. Using multivariate analytical techniques, the researchers reported that the experimental LC had a significant impact on the first-year students' gains in measures of intellectual and personal development, sense of community in the first year, and—most important—persistence.

NEW DIRECTIONS FOR INSTITUTIONAL RESEARCH • DOI: 10.1002/ir

Baker and Pomerantz (2000) examined the impact of an LC program for nontraditional first-year students at a public commuter institution. The authors suggested that LCs provide a value-added component that includes opportunities for students to form bonds with one another and to have increased interaction with faculty. The LC program was based on a course clustering model that included twenty-five students taking the same three courses together. The 328 students who were participating in the LC program were compared to 328 non-LC students on the following outcomes: GPA, retention from fall to spring, credit hours earned, percentage on probation, percentage on the honors or dean's list, and the total number of courses dropped.

Baker and Pomerantz examined both persistence in each of the classes in which students were enrolled as well as persistence between semesters. In this highly rigorous study, the researchers found that the LC group was less likely (only 4 percent) to leave classes within the semester, as opposed to those who were in the control group (9 percent). These differences were significant at the .05 level. No differences were found in the persistence rates of LC participants and nonparticipants across two semesters. However, the LC had an impact on fall GPAs (2.61 compared to 2.34 for the control group, significant at the .002 level), semester hours earned (10.62 compared to 9.54 for the control group, significant at the .004 level), and numbers of students on probation in the LC ($n = 33$) and the control ($n = 54$) groups (11 percent for the LC group and 17 percent for the control group, significant at the .05 level). Consequently, the authors concluded that the LC had an impact on several factors that indirectly and positively affected long-term retention.

Johnson and Romanoff (1999) explored the Russell Scholars Program (RSP), a residential learning community at University of Southern Maine that encouraged faculty and peer interactions for strong students. Students were required to take three courses specific to the learning community. They also received mentoring and were able to have frequent contact with faculty members. Research was conducted during the first year of the program on thirty program participants (fourteen male, sixteen female). Participants were asked to complete background questionnaires and the Johnson Learner Preference Scale (JLPS). A randomly selected sample of students from the general university population served as a matched control group of non-Russell Scholars. The researchers found that Russell Scholars were more pleased with their experiences with faculty and resources and with their overall experience at the university. The least important concern for the students was working to complete courses in order to transfer to another university. Because this investigation had a small sample, it was classified as a study of low rigor. This study did not speak specifically about retention. However, because students noted that transferring was not a concern, we were led to conclude that the program was beneficial for student retention.

The Coordinated Studies Program (CSP) is another form of an LC, housed at a northwestern metropolitan community college that allows students to register for a cluster of courses. In this study by Tinto and Russo

(1994), judged to be of high rigor, the authors administered two question-naires at the beginning of the first year and later during the first year to a panel of program students and a panel of nonprogram students. The sample of 287 students included 121 program students and 166 students in the nonprogram comparison group. The qualitative methods included participant observation and interviews of program participants and staff over the course of the year.

The class met between eleven and eighteen hours each week in blocks of four to six hours over two to four days, was team-taught by two to four faculty members, and was organized around a theme that links the courses from different disciplines and fields. Tinto and Russo found that CSP students reported greater involvement in both academic and social activities, which led to greater developmental gains than the nonprogram participants. CSP students persisted at a higher rate than similar non-CSP students, and this difference in persistence occurred in the following spring and fall quarters. More specifically, the CSP students' persistence rate for the spring was 83.8 percent (versus 80.9 percent for the control group); persistence in the fall was 66.7 percent for the CSP group (versus 52 percent for the control group) and both results were significant at the .05 level.

A final example of a structured course is the Gateway program, which is housed at a large public institution in the northeast. The study of this program (Gebelt and Parilis, 1996) was a large-sample study of moderate rigor that included data from 460 participants. Those students who remained in college for two years were considered persisters.

Developed for first-year students whose scores on the New Jersey College Basic Skills Test (NJCBST) and SAT scores warrant placing them in developmental classes, the program offers a structured learning environment for at-risk students. Based on a student's weakness in particular areas of the NJCBST, he or she was assigned to the appropriate developmental Gateway course. In their study, Gebelt and Parilis evaluated the impact of the Gateway Psychology course and its impact on retention from fall 1991 through spring 1994 to determine the extent to which these students persisted at the same rate as non-Gateway general psychology students. The authors noted that because almost all students are enrolled in the remedial English component, there was no way to have a control group.

Participants in the Gateway course persisted at a rate of 78.7 percent compared to 82.7 percent ($p = .13$) for non-Gateway students. Essentially, no significant differences emerged between Gateway and non-Gateway students in terms of graduation rates. However, the authors did find a significant difference in persistence (at the $p < .001$ level) for those who continued to be enrolled at the institution but had not yet graduated.

Looking across these studies, we were again struck by the fact that there were not more published studies of the impact of learning communities and structured courses on student retention. Learning communities have received a great deal of positive attention, but we found few rigorous assessments of their impact on student persistence. Overall, these studies did present linkages between participation in these courses and persistence. Also, most of these studies were highly rigorous. For this group of published research, the results suggest that learning communities and related structured courses have at least a moderate positive effect on student persistence.

Student-Faculty Interaction. Several scholars in the field of higher education have emphasized the impact of student-faculty interaction (Astin, 1993; Pascarella and Terenzini, 1977, 1980b; Tinto, 1993). Posited as a form of academic integration (Tinto, 1987), the concept of student-faculty interaction espouses both in-class and out-of-class activities with faculty members as a method of facilitating the development of meaningful relationships between students and their professors, which in turn enhances persistence. We found only a small number (three) of empirical evaluations of programmatic interventions designed to enhance student and faculty interaction to improve student persistence.

Craft (2001) conducted a low-rigor study of the South Carolina Advanced Technological (SCATE) program. The first phase of the program included faculty development initiatives that provided extensive training. The goal was to move faculty out of their discipline-specific silos and encourage active learning environments as exemplified in the workplace. Another aspect of the program included a component of faculty and student teams. Unfortunately, the author used only descriptive statistics to assess the impact on retention and did not include a control group, so the efficacy of the program could not be determined.

The Adventor program at Kutztown University targeted the needs of incoming students of color and the barriers they encountered in completing their degrees. The study used a small sample consisting of nineteen students and fifteen faculty members. There was a control group, but it is not described. The program required students to interact with their advisers on a weekly basis (such as e-mail messages, visits, phone calls, and so on) and to maintain consistent contact (Schultz, Colton, and Colton, 2001). This study of low rigor summarized data collected during the program's first year. Although the authors did not explain the kinds of analyses they conducted on the data, they reported that 77 percent of the program's participants returned for a second year, while only 67 percent of the control group returned (but no level of significance was provided).

Nagda and others (1998) conducted a study rated to be of moderate rigor of the Undergraduate Research Opportunities Program (UROP), which was designed to facilitate relationship building between students and faculty by creating undergraduate research partnerships. In this study, 1,280 African American, Hispanic, and white first-year students and sophomores served as participants. A stratified random sampling method was used to select students from a pool of 2,873 program applicants. Then, students were assigned to control and experimental groups based on a matched random assignment. The experimental group consisted of 613 students who participated in the program and the control group consisted of 667 students who were not program participants. Core program components included common matriculation time into the program; peer advising; peer research interest groups; faculty to serve as sponsors; a mutual-selection process between student and faculty sponsor; student research presentations; and academic credit and assessment. The faculty component facilitated regular contact in an engaging, one-on-one relationship to foster academic competency and academic integration. Participants met individually and regularly with their faculty sponsors.

The most significant impact of this program was on low-achieving African American students, as evidenced by their attrition rate of 15.3 percent versus that of the control group's 27.1 percent (significant at the <.07 level). Surprisingly, the researchers also found that the program had a much larger impact on sophomores (attrition rate of 4.3 percent versus 9.5 percent for the control group, significant at the $p = .03$ level) than on first-year students (there was no significant impact on the entire sample of UROP participants).

In total, these studies provide consistent, positive support for the assertion that student persistence can be enhanced by developing campus-based initiatives that facilitate student-faculty interaction. As a group, these articles further illustrate the need to research the positive impact that faculty contact has on student retention. Once again, however, with only a small number of published studies and a dearth of highly rigorous studies, we conclude that there is only moderate support for this proposition.

Transition Programs. College transition programs, often referred to as orientation programs, are a common student-retention initiative at colleges and universities (Titley, 1985). According to Overland and Rentz (2004), "For as long as new students have experienced a period of transition to the educational environment, orientation programs have been a part of American higher education" (p. 239). Orientation and transition programs are designed to help students make the transition from the high school environment to the collegiate environment (Perigo and Upcraft, 1989). They may consist of an overall summer program format; an introductory course; or smaller, individualized programs, such as Welcome Week. In general, most programs have four central goals: to aid students in their academic adjustment; to assist students with personal adjustment; to help families understand college and available services; and to assist the institution in gathering data on incoming students (Overland and Rentz, 2004). Our search for published articles located twenty-five articles for review, but only four articles directly assessed the impact of a transition program on student persistence.

The Summer Fireside Experience Program (SFEP), a supplemental precollege, five-day, adventure-based orientation program ($n = 32$), a Freshman Camp (FC) group ($n = 64$), and a control group ($n = 64$) were evaluated by Gass (1990) and studied over three and a half years. The programs were offered to first-year students at a northeastern public institution. SFEP included a range of outdoor physical activities and team activities that reinforced academic and social goals related to student retention (student development, positive interaction with faculty, career and major development, academic focus, and connection between course offerings and student expectations).

The Freshman Camp participants experienced a four-day program in a residential environment consisting of small-group activities, question-and-answer sessions with upper-class students, interaction with faculty, and school spirit activities. Their follow-up activities consisted of letters from counselors and informal meetings with fellow participants and faculty members. The control group did not participate in either program, nor did they receive any additional orientation beyond the required two-day program. In this study of moderate rigor, attrition data were collected on the three groups both one year and three and a half years after the students entered the institution. The design controlled for high school rank and college aptitude test scores. Retention rates for the SFEP students were 15 percent higher than for the Freshman Camp students and 25 percent higher than the control group for the first twelve months (significant at the .05 level).

In a study of moderate rigor of another transition program, Young, Backer, and Rogers (1989) evaluated the Early Advising and Scheduling System (EASS), which was adopted in the spring of 1986 at a public institution serving twenty-one thousand students. The effectiveness of this program was tested on a population of 2,300 prospective first-year students. The program allowed individuals who had been admitted as first-year students but who had not yet accepted admission to come to campus during the spring semester of their high school senior year for an advising and registration session. The program also provided an orientation to the university for parents. This one-day early orientation program provided students and parents with campus information as well as an opportunity to register early for fall classes.

In this highly rigorous study, the authors measured student attrition from the first year to the second year. The investigators used ACT composite and high school GPA as independent variables and first-year college grades and attrition as criterion variables for all fall 1986 first-year students. Descriptive results suggested that the program had a positive impact on persistence. However, additional multivariate analyses revealed that EASS members scored higher than nonparticipants on the ACT and had higher high school GPAs. Also, they found these differences explained the improved retention rates for EASS, and they concluded that EASS was a predictor of first-year grades at a statistically significant level but was not a predictor of student persistence.

Boyd and others (1997) assessed the impact of the Summer Orientation Parent Transition Program for parents of first-year students attending a large public institution. This investigation included 150 sets of parents who were part of this intervention. Another group of ninety parents went through a different orientation program and served as the control group. This program was designed to equip parents with information about the institution in hopes of enabling them to act as referral agents should their students encounter academic or social difficulties that were inhibiting their ability to be successful students and to persist.

In this study, judged to be of moderate rigor, the authors looked at "academic persistence" (defined as continuous enrollment for a given semester) and "academic persistence in good standing" (being enrolled for a given semester and ending that semester with no negative academic action, such as probation, warning, or dismissal). Although there was no difference in academic persistence among the experimental and control groups, there was a significant difference among the students who were determined to be in academic persistence in good standing. In the fall semester, retention rates for the treatment group were 79 percent versus the comparison group's 63 percent (significant at the $p < .01$ level); in the spring, the rates were 73 percent and 60 percent, respectively (significant at the $p < .05$ level).

Positive effects of a different type of freshman orientation intervention were also found in a study conducted by House and Kuchynka (1997). "University Experience" is an example of what is commonly described as a University 101-type of course. In this instance it was offered at a public institution. This moderately rigorous study included an experimental group consisting of 85 and a control group consisting of 431 first-year students. Students were exposed to opportunities to learn more about their institution and develop more understanding about and interests in their choice of a major. Using a chi-square analysis, the authors found that students who took the course had an 82.4 percent persistence rate (70/85), in comparison to the control group's 64.5 percent (278/483); these results are significant at the $p < .01$ level.

Overall, the studies in this section included more rigorous statistical testing. Thus, we believe that similar studies in this area could lend further support to the assertion that orientation, University 101, and other transition efforts are important for students. Although not every study found strong links to retention, as with other previously mentioned studies, the findings were associated with retention factors such as GPA and academic and social integration.

Conclusions

After mining several electronic databases and reviewing almost one hundred articles, only sixteen studies were identified as providing documentation that links a program with retention. The strength of the connections between programmatic interventions and student persistence varied in these studies. Only in the area of transition programs did we find a reasonable number of studies that reported consistently strong connections between interventions and improved student persistence. Overall, our findings demonstrate that academe is without a core set of documents upon which administrators can rely when seeking retention models to employ at their own institutions. Our analyses of the existing research on programmatic efforts to improve student retention rates lead us to the following substantive conclusions:

The evidence supporting the effectiveness of counseling as a means to reduce dropout rates of undergraduate students is weak.

The evidence to support the efficacy of mentoring programs as a means to reduce dropout rates is weak.

There are small to moderate levels of positive evidence that learning communities have a positive effect on student persistence.

There are small to moderate levels of evidence that programmatic interventions designed to enhance student-faculty interaction can improve student persistence.

There is moderate to strong positive evidence that transition or orientation programs can improve student retention rates.

In addition to these areas, there is a host of areas for which there is simply no evidence to support the effectiveness, or lack thereof, of campus-based retention efforts. Within the body of empirical studies that does exist, the research team found that there is also a lack of longitudinal assessments of retention-based initiatives. The majority of the studies captured the program's impact at a single point in time.

After dissecting the studies, we also found mixed results on various programmatic themes. As we mentioned earlier, the studies' findings were as diverse as the number of programs. We wonder, however, whether an increase in the number of published empirical studies will yield more consistency in the findings. Our findings also revealed other gaps in the retention literature. We found few empirical studies that had been conducted at community colleges or at minority-serving institutions.

Implications

We end this chapter with the same questions with which we began: How do institutions of higher education know that the programs and services that they offer contribute to undergraduate student retention? How do we know that the countless dollars and budgets that are labeled for retention efforts actually work? In the past it was often possible to make claims again and again about the necessity and success of campus retention programs without providing empirical results. However, increasingly campus administrators are asking for evidence as a return on the institution's investment in campus programs.

As a result of our findings, we contend that the present provides an excellent opportunity for colleges and universities to assess the impact of their various programs on retention. The dearth of published empirical studies emphasizes the need to create and promote models for assessing the effectiveness of retention programs. Woodard, Mallory, and De Luca (2001) present a framework for this purpose. There are undoubtedly a number of other viable approaches, but the point is that administrators need a point of reference from which to understand the importance of establishing the groundwork for effectively and efficiently assessing a program; understanding how to identify, capture, and analyze data and communicate findings to various audiences; and understanding how to use the findings to improve the program. We encourage campus administrators and higher education scholars to get involved in evaluating the effectiveness of campus-based retention programs.

References

Andreu, M. L. "Developing and Implementing Local-Level Retention Studies: A Challenge for Community College Institutional Researchers." *Community College Journal of Research and Practice,* 2002, 26(4), 333–344.

Astin, A. W. *Achieving Educational Excellence: A Critical Assessment of Priorities and Practices in Higher Education.* San Francisco: Jossey-Bass, 1985.

Astin, A. W. *What Matters in College: Four Critical Years Revisited.* San Francisco: Jossey Bass, 1993.

Baker, S., and Pomerantz, N. "Impact of Learning Communities on Retention at a Metropolitan University." *Journal of College Student Retention,* 2000, 2(2), 115–126.

Bean, J. "Why Students Leave: Insights from Research." In D. Hossler and J. P. Bean (eds.), *The Strategic Management of College Enrollments.* San Francisco: Jossey-Bass, 1990.

Bifulco, R. "Addressing Self-Selection Bias in Quasi-Experimental Evaluations of Whole-School Reform: A Comparison of Methods." *Evaluation Review,* 2002, 26(5), 545–572.

Boyd, V., and others. "Parents as Referral Agents for Their First-Year College Students: A Retention Intervention." *Journal of College Student Development,* 1997, 38(1), 83–85.

Braxton, J. M., Sullivan, A. S., and Johnson, R. M. "Appraising Tinto's Theory of College Student Departure." In J. C. Smart (ed.), *Higher Education: A Handbook of Theory and Research,* vol. 12. New York: Agathon Press, 1997.

Cabrera, A. F., Stampen, J. O., and Hansen, W. L. "Exploring the Effects of Ability to Pay on Persistence in College." *Review of Higher Education,* 1990, 13(3), 303–336.

Craft, E. "Developing and Implementing an Integrated, Problem-Based Engineering Technology Curriculum in an American Technical College System." *Community College Journal of Research and Practice,* 2001, 25(5/6), 425–440.

Dale, P. M., and Zych, T. "A Successful College Retention Program." *College Student Journal,* 1996, 30(3), 354–360.

Farabaugh-Dorkins, C. *Beginning to Understand Why Older Students Drop Out of College: A Path Analytic Test of the Bean/Metzner Model of Nontraditional Student Attrition.* AIR Professional File, no. 39, 1991, 1–12. (ED 332598)

Gass, M. A. "The Longitudinal Effects of an Adventure Program on the Retention of Students." *Journal of College Student Development,* 1990, 31(1), 33–38.

Gebelt, J. L., and Parilis, G. M. "Retention at a Large University: Combining Skills with Course Content." *Journal of Developmental Education,* 1996, 20(1), 2–8.

Halpin, R. L. "An Application of the Tinto Model to the Analysis of Freshman Persistence in a Community College." *Community College Review,* 1990, 17(4), 22–32.

Himelhoch, C. R., Nichols, A., Ball, S. R., and Black, L. C. "A Comparative Study of the Factors Which Predict Persistence for African American Students at Historically Black Institutions and Predominantly White Institutions." Paper presented at the annual meeting of the Association for the Study of Higher Education, 1997. (ED 415813)

House, J. D., and Kuchynka, S. J. "The Effects of a Freshman Orientation Course on the Achievement of Health Sciences Students." *Journal of College Student Development,* 1997, *38*(5), 540–541.

Hoxby, C. "Would School Choice Change the Teaching Profession?" *Journal of Human Resources,* 2002, *37,* 846–891.

Hurtado, S., and Carter, D. F. "Effects of College Transition and Perceptions of the Campus Racial Climate on Latino College Students' Sense of Belonging." *Sociology of Education,* 1997, *70*(4), 324–345.

Jacobi, M. "Mentoring and Undergraduate Academic Success: A Literature Review." *Review of Educational Research,* 1991, *61*(4), 505–532.

Johnson, C. "Mentoring Programs." In M. L. Upcraft, J. N. Gardner, and Associates (eds.), *The Freshman Year Experience.* San Francisco: Jossey-Bass, 1989.

Johnson, J. L., and Romanoff, S. J. "Higher Education Learning Communities: What Are the Implications for Student Success?" *College Student Journal,* 1999, *33*(3), 385–400.

Mallette, B. I., and Cabrera, A. F. "Determinants of Withdrawal Behavior: An Exploratory Study." *Research in Higher Education,* 1991, *32*(2), 179–194.

Milem, J. F., and Berger, J. B. "A Modified Model of Student Persistence: Exploring the Relationship Between Astin's Theory of Involvement and Tinto's Theory of Student Departure." *Journal of College Student Development,* 1997, *38*(4), 387–400.

Munro, B. H. "Dropouts from Higher Education: Path Analysis of a National Sample." *American Educational Research Journal,* 1981, *18*(2), 133–141.

Nagda, B., and others. "Undergraduate Student-Faculty Research Partnerships Affect Student Retention." *Review of Higher Education,* 1998, *22*(1), 55–72.

Nora, A., Attinasi, L. C., and Matonak, A. "Testing Qualitative Indicators of Precollege Factors in Tinto's Attrition Model: A Community College Student Population." *Review of Higher Education,* 1990, *13*(3), 327–335.

Overland, W. I., and Rentz, A. L. "Orientation." In F.J.D. MacKinnon and Associates (eds.), *Rentz's Student Affairs Practice in Higher Education.* (3rd ed.) Springfield, Ill.: Thomas, 2004.

Pascarella, E., Duby, P. B., and Iverson, B. K. "A Text and Reconceptualization of a Theoretical Model of College Withdrawal in a Commuter Institution Setting." *Sociology of Education,* 1983, *56*(2), 88–100.

Pascarella, E., and Terenzini, P. "Patterns of Student-Faculty Informal Integration Beyond the Classroom and Voluntary Freshman Attrition." *Journal of Higher Education,* 1977, *52,* 197–210.

Pascarella, E., and Terenzini, P. "Predicting Freshman Persistence and Voluntary Dropout Decisions from a Theoretical Model." *Journal of Higher Education,* 1980a, *51*(1), 60–75.

Pascarella, E., and Terenzini, P. "Student-Faculty and Student-Peer Relationships as Mediators of the Structural Effects of Undergraduate Residence Arrangement." *Journal of Educational Research,* 1980b, *73*(6), 343–353.

Pascarella, E., and Terenzini, P. "Predicting Voluntary Freshman Year Persistence/Withdrawal Behavior in a Residential University: A Path Analytic Validation of Tinto's Model." *Journal of Educational Psychology,* 1983, *75*(2), 215–226.

Perigo, D. J., and Upcraft, M. L. "Orientation Programs." In M. L. Upcraft, J. N. Gardner, and Associates (eds.), *The Freshman Year Experience.* San Francisco: Jossey-Bass, 1989.

Schuh, J. H. "Residence Halls." In F.J.D. MacKinnon and Associates (eds.), *Rentz's Student Affairs Practice in Higher Education.* (3rd ed.) Springfield, Ill.: Thomas, 2004.

Schultz, E., Colton, G., and Colton, C. "The Adventor Program: Advisement and Mentoring for Students of Color in Higher Education." *Journal of Humanistic Counseling,* 2001, *40*(2), 208–218.

Stage, F. K. "Motivation, Academic and Social Integration, and the Early Dropout." *American Educational Research Journal,* 1989, *26*(3), 385–402.

Stahl, V. V., and Pavel, D. M. "Assessing the Bean and Metzner Model with Community

College Student Data." Paper presented at the 73rd Annual Meeting of the American Educational Research Association, San Francisco, Calif., 1992. (ED 344639)

Stoeker, J., Pascarella, E. T., and Wolfle, L. M. "Persistence in Higher Education: A Nine-Year Test of a Theoretical Model." *Journal of College Student Development*, 1988, 29(3), 196–209.

Thile, E. I., and Matt, G. E. "The Ethnic Mentor Undergraduate Program: A Brief Description and Preliminary Findings." *Journal of Multicultural Counseling and Development*, 1995, 23(2), 116–127.

Tierney, W. G. "An Anthropological Analysis of Student Participation in College." *Journal of Higher Education*, 1992, 63(6), 603–618.

Tinto, V. *Leaving College: Rethinking the Causes and Cures of Student Attrition*. (1st ed.) Chicago: University of Chicago Press, 1987.

Tinto, V. *Leaving College: Rethinking the Causes and Cures of Student Attrition*. (2nd ed.) Chicago: University of Chicago Press, 1993.

Tinto, V., and Russo, P. "Coordinated Studies Programs: Their Effect on Student Involvement at a Community College." *Community College Review*, 1994, 22(2), 16–26.

Titley, B. S. "Orientation Programs." In L. Noel, R. Levitz, D. Saluri, and Associates (eds.), *Increasing Student Retention*. San Francisco: Jossey-Bass, 1985.

Turner, A. L., and Berry, T. R. "Counseling Center Contributions to Student Retention and Graduation: A Longitudinal Assessment." *Journal of College Student Development*, 2000, 41(6), 627–636.

Williamson, D. R., and Creamer, D. C. "Student Attrition in Two- and Four-Year Colleges: Application of a Theoretical Model." *Journal of College Student Development*, 1988, 29(3), 210–217.

Wilson, S. B., Mason, T. W., and Ewing, M.J.M. "Evaluating the Impact of Receiving University-Based Counseling Services on Student Retention." *Journal of Counseling Psychology*, 1997, 44(3), 316–320.

Woodard, D. B., Jr., Mallory, S. L., and De Luca, A. M. "Retention and Institutional Effort: A Self-Study Framework." *NASPA Journal*, 2001, 39(1), 53–83.

Young, R. B., Backer, R., and Rogers, G. "The Impact of Early Advising and Scheduling on Freshman Success." *Journal of College Student Development*, 1989, 30, 309–312.

LORI D. PATTON is assistant professor in the Higher Education Program at Iowa State University. Her areas of expertise include students of color in higher education, cultural centers on predominantly white campuses, and college student retention.

CARLA MORELON received her Ph.D. in higher education and student affairs from Indiana University. Her areas of interest include access, accreditation, enrollment management, institutional effectiveness, strategic planning, and student engagement.

DAWN MICHELE WHITEHEAD is a doctoral candidate in education policy studies at Indiana University. Her areas of interest include international and comparative education, teacher training, and African Studies.

DON HOSSLER is professor of educational leadership and policy studies at Indiana University and director of the Project on Academic Success, a set of funded studies focusing on how campuses can enhance student success and persistence.

2

In spite of substantial investment in retention in Indiana higher education, there have been only a few well-designed studies that evaluate the effects of these interventions.

Cataloging Institutional Efforts to Understand and Reduce College Student Departure

John M. Braxton, Jeffrey S. McKinney, Pauline J. Reynolds

College going, college persistence, and college success are of continuing and increasing concern for all educators in the United States. Indiana is no different, particularly for a state where a small proportion of residents have bachelor's degrees, perhaps due to the legacy of educational inopportunity or the impact of the "brain drain" syndrome (National Center for Public Policy and Higher Education, 2004). In this context, as is demonstrated by the findings of Measuring Up 2004 (National Center for Public Policy and Higher Education, 2004), the numbers of students from the state going to college and graduating have potentially a greater impact on its prosperity, which is a social and economic incentive for improving participation and persistence in higher education.

According to the Indiana Higher Education Overview by the Indiana Commission for Higher Education (ICHE) (2003), the participation of students in higher education has improved in the state over the last ten years. However, the retention of these students is now of concern, especially for minority students. Data compiled by ICHE from the state's institutions of postsecondary education is illustrative of the situation in Indiana. In 2000, ICHE reported, 60 percent of Indiana's high school graduates enrolled the next fall semester in postsecondary education. The following year, 2001, 76.9 percent of the first-year students at four-year colleges enrolled for their second year, but only 46.1 percent of students at two-year institutions

NEW DIRECTIONS FOR INSTITUTIONAL RESEARCH, no. 130, Summer 2006 © Wiley Periodicals, Inc.
Published online in Wiley InterScience (www.interscience.wiley.com) • DOI: 10.1002/ir.177

returned for their second year. A longitudinal perspective presents a more worrisome situation. Although above the national average, in 2002, only 54.2 percent of the students who enrolled in Indiana institutions as first-year students in 1996 had completed their baccalaureate degrees. Of even more concern is that only 24 percent of African American students and 36 percent of Hispanic students completed and attained their degrees during this period, as depicted in the Indiana Higher Education Overview (ICHE, 2003).

Recent statewide steps to increase the adequate preparation of students as they enter postsecondary institutions include a reformed high school curriculum option available at some schools, called Core 40, which state legislators hope will take over regular diplomas and is part of a P–16 plan for the state. Statewide transfer and articulation agreements between institutions of postsecondary education have been implemented to ease and improve transfer of students in the state, and bolstering and increasing financial support to the state community college have increased the options of students (ICHE, 2003).

During the past five years, the Lilly Endowment and the Lumina Foundation for Education have aided both public and private institutions in the state of Indiana by providing grants to support the development of new programs aimed at improving the success and retention of college students. A diverse range of programs and services has been developed during this period. Indiana, by many accounts, has become a national leader in the field of student access, success, and retention, especially compared to similar states in the country. An additional positive development has been the creation of a community of practitioners and researchers who are knowledgeable about student access and retention.

These statewide efforts, coupled with concern about the retention of students, provided the impetus for the Indiana Project on Retention (IPR) to commission the research described in this chapter. The IPR is funded by a grant from Lumina Foundation for Education. It is ostensibly a planning project designed to ascertain the needs and condition of Indiana's institutions of higher education regarding the retention and success of their students. Through conversations, interactions, and conferences involving representatives invited from all the institutions in the state, the project seeks to determine if there is a viable need for a statewide initiative focused on retention and success.

One purpose of the project is to explore the nexus between research and practice. For example, we asked the following question: Is the latest work completed by researchers on student persistence and success incorporated by those practitioners in the field who are working closely with students? During a statewide conference and conversation in February 2003, colleges and universities became more interested in how successful Indiana institutions were in retaining their students. From this conference, IPR staff, in consultation with John Braxton, began to seek information from all of the colleges and universities in the state of Indiana.

NEW DIRECTIONS FOR INSTITUTIONAL RESEARCH • DOI: 10.1002/ir

The IPR posits its major purpose as the creation of new avenues for improving student success in Indiana. Student retention provides a significant gateway to student success. An inventory of retention programming by colleges and universities in Indiana constitutes one of the major activities under the aegis of the IPR performed to increase student success by increasing the likelihood of student retention. Accordingly, this chapter reports our efforts in cataloging institutional efforts to understand and reduce college student departure in colleges and universities in the state of Indiana.

This process entailed collecting the results of research studies on retention that individual colleges and universities in the state of Indiana have conducted to understand student retention at their institution. A focus on the efforts of one state engaged in understanding and reducing college student departure may frame questions for examining the efforts of other states.

Colleges and universities in Indiana were asked to provide the project team with written reports of such studies and accompanying materials (surveys, statistical tables, and so on). We initially sent out forty-seven requests to campuses in Indiana. After subsequent phone calls and messages, thirty-six institutions responded in some way. We ultimately received materials from twenty-two campuses. From these institutions, relevant materials were provided by sixteen colleges and universities. These sixteen collegiate institutions provided thirty-four documents of various types. Some institutions provided more than one document.

Classification of Retention-Related Materials

We classified the thirty-four documents provided by sixteen colleges and universities in the state of Indiana into four categories: institutional studies, assessments of programs designed to reduce student departure, assessments of the college environment and experience, and reports of policies and programs developed to reduce student departure.

Institutional Studies. Within the category of institutional studies, we identified five types of studies seeking an understanding of institutional student retention: multivariate studies, bivariate studies, percentage comparisons on various factors between retained and nonretained students, autopsy studies, and descriptions of institutional rates of departure. Of the thirty-four documents received, we classified nineteen of them as one of these five types of studies.

These types of studies vary on a continuum of methodological and statistical rigor, with multivariate studies being the most rigorous and descriptions of institutional rates of departure being the least rigorous. Inferences about the process of student departure at a given college or university result from multivariate studies. Although the other three types of studies yield weak inferences, such studies offer leads for future research about student departure at a given college or university.

NEW DIRECTIONS FOR INSTITUTIONAL RESEARCH • DOI: 10.1002/ir

Of the nineteen documents describing institutional studies, seven fit the category of multivariate studies. Of these seven multivariate studies, four were conducted over a period of several years at the same university. However, only two of these multivariate studies used some semblance of a theoretical foundation. Specifically, these two documents include in their multivariate statistical analyses factors indicative of student participation in campus life—a proxy indicator for social integration. Social integration constitutes a core construct of Tinto's interactionalist theory of college student departure (Braxton, Hirschy, and McClendon, 2004). The interactionalist perspective holds as important the interaction of the student with the academic and social communities of a college or university. Although high school academic achievement is a student entry characteristic included in Tinto's theory, it is not a core construct to the interactionalist perspective.

We grouped the remaining twelve documents classified as institutional studies into four distinct types within the broader category of institutional studies. Two documents report bivariate or zero-order relationships between selected factors posited as being associated with student retention. Three documents report comparisons of the percentage of retained and nonretained students on various student characteristics and other factors posited to be related to student retention. These percentage comparisons are reported without the warrant of tests of statistical significance. Three other documents report the results of interviews or surveys of students who had withdrawn from the focal college or university. Such studies, termed autopsies, lack methodological rigor, as the factors identified as related to departure by withdrawn students may also apply to students who continue to be enrolled (Braxton, Brier, and Hossler, 1988; Terenzini, 1982). Finally, four reports of institutional rates of departure by various groups of students were supplied.

Assessments of Student Departure Reduction Programs. Pascarella (1986) urges colleges and universities to test the efficacy of campus-based intervention programs designed to reduce student departure. Of the thirty-four documents supplied, six documents report the results of assessments of institutional programs developed to reduce student departure at their college or university. Five different colleges and universities in the state of Indiana supplied a report describing the results of their appraisal of one or more programs designed directly or indirectly to retain students at their college or university. The programs assessed included a summer success program, learning communities, an advisor training program, and a set of initiatives designed to ease the transition to college.

Intervention programs that reduce the rate of student departure include learning communities, first-year residence halls, and student mentoring provided for difficult courses. According to a report supplied, student participation in learning communities at one Indiana public university reduced the likelihood of student departure. At this same university, the assignment of students to live in a residence hall for first-year students also increased their rate of retention. A report provided by another public university described interviews with students who participated in a learning community, offering a perspective on the efficacy of learning communities in student retention. This report indicates that students perceived their academic and social opportunities to be richer in learning communities than in their other courses at this university.

Student mentoring also tended to increase student retention, as reported in a document submitted by a third Indiana public university. Peer mentoring entails assigning students to a student mentor who helps them learn difficult course material. Such mentors receive training in the learning process.

Assessments of the College Environment and Experience. Assessing the environment or subenvironments of a college or university can shed light on the types of interactions students may encounter with the institution or segments within the institution. Such an understanding, when coupled with the results of an institutional retention study, may further an understanding of the college student departure process at a given college or university. Four documents report the findings of appraisals of the college environment or subenvironments at three different colleges and universities.

These appraisals include a survey of student satisfaction with a range of such institutional factors as academic advising, campus climate, campus life, registration effectiveness, instructional effectiveness, responsiveness to diverse populations, and campus support services. Another document reports the results of an assessment of the environments of residence halls as perceived by first-year students. A third document reports the results of focus groups discussing factors in college choice, surprises about the institution, aspects that were going well, frustrations, social life, and the possibility of departure. The fourth document reports a survey conducted of current students that focused on such factors as their attitudes about the institution's quality and image, type of courses and course scheduling, and social life at the institution.

Reports of Student Departure Reduction Policies and Programs. Of the thirty-four documents received, five report policies and programs proposed or enacted by the focal college or university. Five different colleges and universities provided such a report.

Conclusions and Recommendations

Two limitations temper the conclusions and recommendations for practice we advance. First, slightly more than one-third (34 percent) of the colleges and universities in the state of Indiana responded to our request for written reports and accompanying materials pertinent to retention. A greater rate of participation might result in different categories to classify retention-related documents or in a change in the distribution of documents within the four categories we developed. Second, we developed our categories and subcategories based on a reading of the documents supplied. Consequently, we are unable to classify any activities or statistical procedures not described in the documents given us.

NEW DIRECTIONS FOR INSTITUTIONAL RESEARCH • DOI: 10.1002/ir

Conclusions for State-Level and Institutional Policymakers. Four conclusions emerge from the findings of this chapter. Although these conclusions apply to colleges and universities in the state of Indiana, the policymakers and institutional leaders of colleges and universities in other states should find these conclusions provocative. These conclusions frame the type of questions state-level and institutional policymakers in states other than Indiana should pursue.

1. As indexed by the thirty-four documents supplied by sixteen colleges and universities in the state of Indiana, these colleges and universities have invested some institutional resources and effort into understanding and reducing student departure at their institutions. This level of activity around retention raises a serious question about the efforts of the thirty-one Indiana colleges and universities that did not respond to this project's request for materials.
2. The vast majority of colleges and universities in Indiana have not conducted campus-based retention studies of sufficient methodological and statistical rigor. This conclusion stems from the finding of this report that seven of thirty-four documents report multivariate statistical procedures used to determine the influence of various factors on college student departure. For each college and university to understand and reduce its own rates of student departure, each individual college and university should conduct studies of sufficient methodological and statistical rigor.
3. Based on the findings of this report, "extremely rare" best describes the use of theories of college student departure, as only two documents out of thirty-four use concepts derived from theory. This condition occurs despite the array of theoretical perspectives available to guide institutionally based studies of college student departure.
4. The National Report Card issued by the National Center for Public Policy and Higher Education (2004) gives the state of Indiana a grade of B for completion of degrees and certificates. Future progress on this indicator seems unlikely unless more public and private colleges and universities in the state conduct studies of student departure at their institutions that are theory-driven and methodologically and statistically rigorous. Such studies provide sound bases for policies and practices designed to reduce institutional rates of student departure.

Recommendations for Policy and Practice. We also advance four recommendations for policy and practice that emerge from the contents of this chapter. These recommendations apply not only to the state of Indiana but to the other forty-nine states as well. The first two recommendations posit standards for the execution of institutionally based studies of college student departure and for research and development on policies, programs, and practices designed to increase student retention.

1. All individual colleges and universities in Indiana as well as in other states should conduct studies of student departure. When possible, such studies should be guided by theory and should employ multivariate statistical procedures to determine the influence of various factors on student departure. Institutional research officers or other individuals charged with the responsibility of conducting such studies should select theoretical perspectives best suited to explain student departure at their type of college or university. Braxton, Hirschy, and McClendon (2004) contend that, because commuter colleges and universities lack well-structured and well-defined social communities, the study of departure in these institutions requires theoretical formulations different from those used to account for departure from residential colleges and universities. Those authors put forth a substantial revision of Tinto's interactionalist theory to explain student departure from residential colleges and universities and propose a new theory to account for departure from two-year and four-year commuter institutions. Institutional research officers or other individuals responsible for conducting a campus-based retention study should consider using these two theories.

2. Following the recommendations of Pascarella (1986), research and development focused on the identification of efficacious policies and programs designed to reduce institutional rates of student departure should take place at individual colleges and universities in Indiana as well as other states. As indicated in this chapter, five Indiana colleges and universities have appraised the effectiveness of programs designed to reduce student departure. Colleges and universities in Indiana and the other states should use research and evaluation to inform change on their campuses. Evaluation and assessment of these programs should be integral to the planning process.

3. In Indiana and other states, colleges and universities should build the capacity for institutional research on their campuses, especially regional campuses and two-year institutions. Given the findings of this current study, building this capacity is crucial for understanding the success and retention of college students.

4. The research staffs of state-level consolidated governing boards or statewide coordinating boards of states receiving a grade of B or lower on completion from the National Report Card for Higher Education (National Center for Public Policy and Higher Education, 2004) should conduct inventories of institutional efforts to reduce student departure similar to the project reported in this chapter. Particular emphasis should be placed on the collection of research studies on retention that individual colleges and universities in these states have conducted to understand student retention at their institutions. Although we recommended this for states receiving a grade of B or lower, we consider it imperative for the seventeen states receiving grades of C or lower.

NEW DIRECTIONS FOR INSTITUTIONAL RESEARCH • DOI: 10.1002/ir

Concluding Thoughts

College student departure occupies the attention and concern of institutional practitioners, state policymakers, and scholars. For more than seventy years, departure has been the object of empirical research, and institutional programs have been developed to reduce departure (Braxton, Hirschy, and McClendon, 2004). In addition, national conferences focusing on reducing student departure have been held. Despite considerable national attention devoted to understanding and reducing college student departure, many colleges and universities in Indiana appear not engaged in the process of understanding and reducing departure at their institutions. This raises a question: Do colleges and universities in other states demonstrate so little effort? To answer this question, the four recommendations advanced in this chapter are particularly important, and we strongly urge their implementation.

References

Braxton, J. M., Brier, E. M., and Hossler, D. "The Influence of Student Problems on Student Withdrawal Decisions: An Autopsy on 'Autopsy' Studies." *Research in Higher Education,* 1988, *28,* 241–253.
Braxton, J. M., Hirschy, A. S., and McClendon, S. A. *Understanding and Reducing College Student Departure.* ASHE-ERIC Higher Education Report, vol. 30, no. 3. San Francisco: Jossey-Bass, 2004.
Indiana Commission for Higher Education (ICHE). "Indiana Higher Education Overview." Paper presented at Indiana's Education Roundtable, May 22, 2003. http://www.che.state.in.us/reportsandstudies. Accessed July 20, 2005.
National Center for Public Policy and Higher Education. "Measuring Up 2004: The National Report Card for Higher Education." San Jose, Calif.: National Center for Public Policy and Higher Education, 2004.
Pascarella, E. T. "A Program of Research and Policy Development on Student Persistence at the Institutional Level." *Journal of College Student Personnel,* 1986, *27,* 100–107.
Terenzini, P. T. "Designing Attrition Studies." In E. T. Pascarella (ed.), *Studying Student Attrition.* New Directions for Institutional Research, no. 36. San Francisco: Jossey-Bass, 1982.

JOHN M. BRAXTON is professor of education in the Higher Education Leadership and Policy Program, Peabody College, Vanderbilt University. One of his major programs of research centers on the college student experience, with particular emphasis on student departure.

JEFFREY S. MCKINNEY is associate director of the Indiana Project on Academic Success. He holds a Ph.D. in higher education and student affairs from Indiana University.

PAULINE J. REYNOLDS is research associate for the Indiana Project on Academic Success at Indiana University.

3

Research on retention of students of color suggests possible areas of intervention to improve academic success.

Key Issues in the Persistence of Underrepresented Minority Students

Deborah Faye Carter

There is a gap between ethnic minority students and ethnic majority students in the attainment of higher education degrees (Allen, 1992; DesJardins, Ahlburg, and McCall, 2002; Hatch and Mommsen, 1984; Mehan, Hubbard, and Villanueva, 1994; Myers, 2003; Pathways to College Network, 2003). Racial or ethnic minority students have a higher probability of leaving post-secondary education than ethnic majority students. This is a serious, long-term problem, as there are growing numbers of students of color in the K–12 student population and they disproportionately are not graduating from college (Keller, 2001; Pascarella and Terenzini, 1998). The Pathways to College Network (2003) reports that when comparing groups of individuals in their late twenties, more than one-third of whites have at least a bachelor's degree, but only 18 percent of African Americans and 10 percent of Hispanics have attained bachelor's degrees.

The gap between underrepresented minority students and other groups is particularly detrimental because it affects individuals' long-term social mobility. The attainment of any postsecondary degree (particularly a baccalaureate degree) often results in a greater net dividend for minority populations (Malveaux, 2003). For example, the median African American family income is 63 percent of the median white family income ("Holding a Four-Year College Degree," 2005). If income data are analyzed only for individuals who received baccalaureate degrees, however, African Americans on average earn 95 percent of what white individuals earn ("Holding," 2005).

NEW DIRECTIONS FOR INSTITUTIONAL RESEARCH, no. 130, Summer 2006   © Wiley Periodicals, Inc.
Published online in Wiley InterScience (www.interscience.wiley.com) • DOI: 10.1002/ir.178

These statistics highlight the necessity of understanding retention issues, especially for underrepresented students. Understanding student retention is not only important for campus leaders, practitioners, and researchers, but it also has long-term effects on society. Nearly twenty years ago, Stewart (1988) asserted that the most urgent need in higher education was the successful participation or retention of minority students. This observation remains true today.

This chapter reviews the general literature relating to the academic success and persistence of minority students. The issues covered in this chapter are of particular interest to institutional researchers for several reasons. First, institutional research (IR) professionals may be called upon or be interested in analyzing student performance (for example, academic achievement, persistence, and retention issues) by racial or ethnic group. Second, institutional administrators may be interested in increasing racial or ethnic diversity in their student populations; the expertise of IR professionals can be critical in assisting with these goals. Data produced in institutional research offices can help ascertain why students from different regions or sociocultural backgrounds choose to attend a particular institution, what academic majors they pursue, and the impact of financial aid on persistence and other educational outcomes.

In this chapter, I begin with a discussion of a statewide study of college student retention issues. The rest of the chapter reviews important literature streams that are generally relevant to understanding retention issues and specifically relevant for underrepresented minority students. The chapter concludes with a discussion of implications for future research.

Retention in a State Context

St. John, Carter, Chung, and Musoba (forthcoming) examined the factors affecting African American, Hispanic, and white students' persistence at public and private institutions in Indiana. The results of the study revealed substantial similarities and a few very important differences in the factors that influence the persistence of the three racial or ethnic groups. The differences between groups are most easily understood if viewed in relation to differences in the situated contexts of the lives of college students, an alternative to the more usual vantage point of seeking to uncover universal patterns across groups of students (Braxton, 2000; Pascarella and Terenzini, 1991). By uncovering differences in persistence patterns across diverse groups, we can illuminate factors that inhibit equal opportunity as well as policy factors that might be able to improve opportunity.

First, background variables were associated with persistence for all three groups in the St. John study, but with substantially different patterns. For whites, having parents who had not attained a college education decreased the odds of academic success in college, while being from families with high incomes improved these odds. For Hispanics and African

NEW DIRECTIONS FOR INSTITUTIONAL RESEARCH • DOI: 10.1002/ir

Americans, high income was a positive factor, but parents' education was not significant. For the three groups, there was a strong relationship between socioeconomic status and student persistence in college. For African Americans and Hispanics, having an adequate aid guarantee enabled students to overcome the barriers related to parents' education and income, a condition that is not met nationally.

A second major area of the study was the role of high school curricula in student persistence rates. The Indiana state context plays a role in how students persist: the study took place in a state that has made an effort to place college preparatory curricula in all high schools. For all three groups, completing preparatory or honors curricula had a sustained positive influence on persistence. High school grades did not have as substantial an influence for white students and had no significant relationship for African American or Hispanic students, indicating that a main academic effort for increasing persistence for students of color may be in the area of increasing the availability of advanced courses.

Third, increasing the availability of advanced courses not only has an effect on college student persistence, but taking advanced courses is associated with high SAT scores in Indiana. However, the effect of taking the SAT had little impact on student persistence for any group. The lack of significance of the SAT on students' college persistence may be because this study took place in a state in which the majority of high school students take the SAT.

Fourth, college choices influenced persistence for white and African American students. Attending state universities, private colleges, and research universities was consistently and positively associated with persistence compared to enrollment in two-year colleges; on the other hand, attending regional campuses, the urban campus, and private colleges did not have this positive association for whites.

There were substantial differences in the association between choice of major and persistence across the three groups. For whites, having a declared major was consistently and positively associated with persistence. However, for African Americans, several academic majors were negatively associated with persistence, and there were no positive associations. These findings raise questions about engagement in academic programs and whether the content of majors meets the expectations of African Americans. Faculties in health, business, education, and computer science in particular need to consider why their majors do not support persistence by diverse students.

In addition to major, there were many common patterns in the effects of college experiences across the three sets of analyses. High college grades were positively associated with persistence and low grades were negatively associated with this outcome in all three analyses. In addition, taking remedial courses in both language and math were consistently and positively associated with persistence. This means that achievement is important, but support services can help students who have special additional needs.

NEW DIRECTIONS FOR INSTITUTIONAL RESEARCH • DOI: 10.1002/ir

Finally, there were differences in the effects of student financial aid across racial or ethnic groups in the state, at least for the entering collegiate class of 2000. For whites and Hispanics there were no significant financial aid variables, suggesting aid may be helping to equalize opportunity, yet high-income students were more likely to persist in all three ethnic groups. Specifically, for African Americans, a group with a high percentage of low-income students, all types of packages with grant aid, including loans and grants, were positively associated with persistence. For Hispanics, receiving packages with work-study substantially improved the odds of persistence, a pattern consonant with a working-class pattern of student choice.

It is apparent that public finance policies do influence different groups in different ways. Because of their high poverty rate in the state, African Americans can benefit from the state's achievement program more than whites. Further, excessive loans can be problematic for middle-income families, who may question whether their expected earnings will grow sufficiently to justify continued borrowing. At the very least, these differences merit further and wider consideration, given the ongoing challenges facing educational opportunity for high-achieving students of color.

Tinto's Model

Tinto's model of student departure (1982, 1993) has been the theoretical framework used most often in examining the predictors of attainment and persistence. Building on the research of Spady (1970, 1971), Tinto proposed a model of student departure that was initially based on the sociological concept of suicide as proposed by Durkheim (1951). Tinto (1993) incorporated Van Gennep's ideas regarding rites of passage (Van Gennep, 1960, as cited by Tinto [1993]) into adulthood in tribal societies into his model in later explorations of student departure. He drew analogies between the concepts of suicide and the passage to adulthood and college student dropout and persistence.

Research using Tinto's framework has contributed a great deal to the understanding of what affects student dropout or departure and student persistence. Several researchers have recognized the utility of the Tinto model in predicting college student attrition (Getzlaf, Sedlacek, Kearney, and Blackwell, 1984; Pascarella and Terenzini, 1980). Tinto (1993) proposed that the occurrence of college student departure provides a window on the social and academic communities in which students experience colleges and universities.

Perspectives on Tinto's Model

Researchers have built on Tinto's model and have offered a variety of different perspectives through which to examine student departure. Some have proposed an examination of student attrition through an organizational perspective. Bean (1980) challenged Tinto's ideas of tying student departure to suicide and proposed that researchers interested in student departure turn to organizational studies that have examined why individuals leave work or group settings. More recently, Bean and Eaton (2000), claiming that the factors affecting retention are related to individual psychological processes involved in developing academic and social integration, developed a psychological model of college student retention. Examples of successful retention programs are learning communities, first-year interest groups, tutoring, mentoring, and student orientation (Myers, 2003).

Over the years, researchers have challenged Tinto's model for its limited applicability to minority students (Braxton, Sullivan, and Johnson, 1997; Tierney, 1992). The researchers have asked those studying student departure to examine carefully the applicability of the Tinto model to the variety of students that are part of higher education today.

Braxton and his colleagues (1997) addressed the fifteen testable propositions derived from Tinto's model in terms of aggregated support, support by institutional type, and support by student group. They proposed that, in the future, researchers may want to assess the fifteen propositions using different student racial or ethnic groups. According to these researchers, "the empirical internal consistency of Tinto's theory is indeterminate for both African Americans and Native Americans/Alaskan natives" (p. 158). They suggested engaging in theory revision or using other theoretical perspectives for studying the retention of racial or ethnic minority-group members.

Tierney (1992) disagrees with the adaptation of anthropological concepts—such as the rituals of transition—into the Tinto model. According to Tierney, "Rituals of transition have never been conceptualized as movements from one culture to another" (p. 611). He maintained that the Tinto model makes assumptions regarding individuals undergoing a rite of passage in a culture that may or may not be their own (such as minority students within white institutions). An additional challenge extended by Tierney is that "essentially, models of integration have the effect of merely inserting minorities into a dominant cultural frame of reference that is transmitted within dominant cultural forms, leaving invisible cultural hierarchies intact" (p. 611).

As a counter to the assumption of integration, in recent years researchers have tried to offer different conceptions of the process by which minority students can successfully navigate predominantly white college environments. Rendón, Jablomo, and Nora (cited in Swail, Redd, and Perna, 2003) describe the process of biculturation whereby students "live simultaneous lives in two cultures, two realities" (p. 49). Troy Duster (also cited in Swail) describes a similar phenomenon as "dual competency" in that "students must be competent in their own culture plus the culture of the institution" (p. 49).

Academic Characteristics

Twenty-five years ago, Thomas (1981) identified some key issues for increasing African American student access and retention in college. High schools, Thomas contended, need to identify earlier and properly support a greater number of college-bound African American students and employ "constructive and earlier use of competency-based testing" (p. 382). Her final recommendation for increasing access to four-year colleges was to increase the role of two-year institutions in promoting the transfer function to four-year institutions and helping students of color have some additional time after high school graduation to increase academic preparation. Thomas's conclusions are similar to the conclusions of researchers in the twenty-first century. Progress has been made in the last two decades, but not nearly as much progress as is needed.

Lavin and Crook (1990) examined ethnic differences in long-term educational attainment and found that minority students demonstrated less academic success all along the way and were far more likely than whites to leave college without any degree. They found that half of the African American and Hispanic students attending community colleges never earned any credentials. African American and Hispanic students receiving diplomas were more likely to earn associate degrees than were whites. In addition, 40 percent of whites went beyond the associate level compared to one-third of African Americans and Hispanics. The authors also found that it typically took minority students longer to earn an undergraduate degree. They concluded that a process of cumulative disadvantage is occurring that is partially derived from differences in high school experience. African Americans and Hispanics reported receiving lower grades in high school and more often came from nonacademic high school tracks.

Allen, Bonous-Hammarth, and Suh (2004) studied student high school preparation, college choice, and factors contributing to college enrollment for students of color. Through the use of quantitative analyses and focus group interviews, the authors "remind[ed] us that educational achievement is a social process, shaped by human exchanges within definitive sociocultural contexts" (p. 96). For example, students described a "tracking" phenomenon whereby students who were designated "smart" were prepared for college, received mentors, and experienced college tours, while the other students received very little assistance in their plans for postsecondary education.

Many students of color experience structural disadvantages, but there are campus academic experiences that affect student outcomes in a positive manner. Hurtado (2001) describes research that links student classroom experiences with diversity-related outcomes. Interaction with diverse student peers and with diverse faculty produce self-reported increases in students' critical thinking skills and writing ability. Hurtado's work has implications for how college campuses structure their classroom learning environments. Colleges can take advantage of peer diversity and train faculty in a variety of pedagogies that can positively affect student outcomes.

College Experiences

Several studies have been done of African American students using surveys and quantitative data analyses. These studies have contributed a great deal of knowledge about the general experiences of African American students across different kinds of colleges and universities, specifically the different experiences of African American students at predominantly white institutions (PWIs) and at historically black colleges and universities (HBCUs).

African American students experience exclusion, racial discrimination, and alienation on predominantly white campuses (Allen, 1992; Turner, 1994). In contrast, at HBCUs, African Americans "emphasize feelings of engagement, connection, acceptance, and . . . encouragement" (Allen, 1992, p. 39). Feagin, Vera, and Imani (1996) detailed some of the negative experiences African Americans have at PWIs. In brief, the African American students felt that white faculty, students, and staff did not view them as "full human beings with distinctive talents, virtues, interests, and problems" (p. 14). Black students at PWIs often feel anxiety and fear at being the only one or one of a few African Americans in a particular environment (Smedley, Myers, and Harrell, 1993). This anxiety can mean that African Americans look for the increased company of other African Americans for their support. Feagin and colleagues also reported that "a recent survey of black students at mostly white universities found they were so concerned about intellectual survival that they were unable to devote as much attention to their personal, social, and cultural development as they should" (p. 75).

Shom and Spooner (1990) investigated several precollegiate programs (for example, Upward Bound and Early Outreach) and concluded that several questions remain regarding the continuing commitment by colleges and universities to monitor and support the educational and maturational progress of the participants and the continuing investment of funds into programs that are involved in this broad initiative of precollegiate programs. They wondered "if this initiative is a case of too little too late to keep pace with the rising tide of minorities who are not being adequately prepared for or stimulated toward a fulfilling experience" (p. 228).

Smedley, Myers, and Harrell (1993) were concerned with the strains of the student role and the stresses of life events and minority status that may affect a student's successful psychological and academic adjustment to college. They report that the "more debilitating minority status stressors were those that undermined students' academic confidence and ability to bond to the university" (p. 448). They found that these stresses come from internal sources as well as from the social climate and composition of the institution.

NEW DIRECTIONS FOR INSTITUTIONAL RESEARCH • DOI: 10.1002/ir

In a study that supports Smedley's research, Bynum and Thompson (1983) examined the issues of student departure at four different institutions. Their findings indicate that students of any race (Native American, African American, or white) who are in the minority on campus are more likely to drop out of college prior to graduation than students in the racial majority.

An inclusive and welcoming institutional environment and the connection of students to that environment have been linked to persistence. Hurtado, Milem, Clayton-Pederson, and Allen (1998) found that the campus climate, or the institutional environment with respect to inclusion, affects the retention of students. According to Kuh (1995), students' connection to the campus environment, often called student engagement, and student involvement are important factors in retaining students. Students who engage on campus may take advantage of more opportunities to secure academic membership and ultimately improve chances of persistence (Bonous-Hammarth, 2000).

Students' in-college experiences have been shown to affect their adjustment to and persistence in college more than do their backgrounds (Hurtado, Carter, and Spuler, 1996). This finding provides hope that retention programs may work to overcome some of the disadvantages of student backgrounds. In a comprehensive review of retention programs, Myers (2003) asserted that the institutional environment has a powerful impact on students' satisfaction with and success in an institution. He elaborated that the institutions that are successful in retaining students are those that are responsive to the academic, social and cultural needs of their students. Tinto (1993) concludes that successful retention programs are longitudinal, are tied to the admissions process, and involve a wide range of institutional actors.

The work of other researchers has also contributed to an understanding of the process of degree attainment. Astin, Tsui, and Avalos (1996) completed a study examining bachelor's degree attainment rates by institutional type. They found that private colleges and universities had significantly higher degree attainment and retention rates than public institutions. They conclude that there are structural elements of postsecondary institutions that independently affect students' attainment levels—despite precollege academic performance levels.

To improve retention, many programs have been successfully employed, among them advising, counseling, tutoring, basic skills development, first-year orientation (Boudreau and Kromrey, 1994), faculty involvement, study skills courses, test-taking clinics, and career advising. Also, residence halls and learning communities on college campuses have demonstrated positive effects on student persistence (Astin, 1993; Berger, 2000; Tinto, 1993).

Student Financial Aid

Access to college and retention in college are two distinct concepts that have been linked in recent research. St. John, Paulsen, and Starkey (1996) first developed the concept of linking issues of access and retention relative to financial aid, and these concepts were expanded in St. John, Paulsen, and Carter (2005). These researchers argued that students choose colleges because of financial reasons and that these financial reasons and the actual college prices have impacts on their college experiences which, in turn, affect persistence. In other words, there is a nexus between students' financial reasons for attending college and their subsequent persistence behavior.

Berger (2000) examined students' patterns of college decision making and related these patterns to socioeconomic status (SES). Indeed, students from different SES groups responded differently to financial aid. Low-income students were more likely to drop out if their levels of grant aid were insufficient, and working-class students were more likely to drop out if their amounts of work-study and loans were not adequate (Paulsen and St. John, 2002).

Previous analyses of differences among racial groups with regard to student aid indicated that African Americans were less likely to persist if financial aid levels were not adequate (Kaltenbaugh, St. John, and Starkey, 1999). In addition, research has indicated that students' college choices are constrained by their social circumstances. For instance, lower SES students tend to be constrained by their financial circumstances in that they attend less expensive institutions closer to their homes (Carter, 1999). This is particularly true for Hispanics, who proportionally have much higher two-year college-going rates than other races or ethnicities.

In addition, researchers have frequently studied the degree to which race and social class affect student access to college. Researchers have concluded that class—more than race—affects student college-going opportunities (Hanson, 1994; Hearn, 1984). However, there are also important racial differences in college access.

An American Council on Education (ACE) study of the "public's knowledge and attitudes about financing higher education" showed that people do not understand the differences between public and private institutions or two-year and four-year colleges (Hartle, 1998). Seventy-one percent of the people surveyed believe that college is not affordable for most families, and 83 percent of the African American respondents believe so.

Recent analyses raise doubts that more information will solve the access problem. The Advisory Committee on Student Financial Assistance (2002) estimates that four million college-qualified low-income and middle-income students will be left behind in the next decade. If finances are a problem in enrollment and persistence, then it is even more important to examine these differences for diverse racial and ethnic groups.

Financial constraints also play a role in attrition (Pathways to College Network, 2003; St. John, 1994). Only one-quarter of low-income students who enroll in postsecondary education actually receive bachelor's degrees (Pathways to College Network, 2003). Financial aid, especially grants, has also been shown to promote persistence. The financial nexus model links college choice and persistence with financial background and need (Paulsen and St. John, 2002). This model asserts that students' perceptions of college costs and the actual dollar amount of costs and aid may affect persistence decisions.

Higher education researchers have shown the enduring effects of SES on college student outcomes (Hearn, 1991). A student's SES is a significant predictor of the type of higher education institution he or she can attend (Pascarella, Smart, and Smylie, 1992). Cabrera, Stampen, and Hansen (1990) addressed the issue of ability to pay on college persistence by expanding Tinto's model by "explicating the potential moderating effects of ability to pay on college persistence" (p. 326). They concluded that ability to pay has a direct effect on college persistence. Some researchers have suggested that the linkage of financial aid to admission strategies is a crucial enrollment management concept (St. John, 1991). This could have particular impact on minority enrollment strategies.

The current struggle to improve the attainments of minority and low-income students comes at a time of increased fiscal pressures in institutions of higher education. Given that state and federal appropriations for higher education have stayed about the same over the past few years, institutions have compensated for the lack of increased government support by increasing tuition. This also has the effect of limiting access to those students who can afford to pay for college. Since minority families tend to have lower incomes than white families (Baker and Vélez, 1991), institutions that strive to make their programs affordable are providing opportunities for increased access and attainment.

Implications

The key areas for minority-student college persistence are academic preparation, adequate financial aid, and strong support networks in college. In years of research on minority students, we have learned quite a lot about the challenges endured by underrepresented populations. However, gaps remain in persistence rates.

Recent research studies on student persistence and minority students have utilized complex statistical techniques and large sample sizes, helping tease out the complexities among the groups and clarify how persistence rates may be differentially affected by similar interventions. It is important that researchers and practitioners continue to design interventions that affect particular populations. Finding best practices for all students may not be serving all students.

Inadvertent discrimination may hinder minority students' progress and may negatively affect their persistence. In the Indiana state study, controlling for preparation, college grades, and remedial courses, African

Americans with majors in business, education, health, and computer science did not persist as well as their peers with undeclared majors. The causes cannot be explained solely by the lack of parental education or low achievement. An atmosphere of inadvertent discrimination may be the case in this state's higher education. The fact that African Americans in several applied majors do not persist as well as their peers with undeclared majors reveals there may be a serious problem with the engagement of the best and brightest minority students. Previous literature has found that minority students do not feel comfortable in college environments that lack diversity. Environments that make minority students feel less than fully human (Feagin, Vera, and Imani, 1996) may be additionally problematic for persistence.

Indiana may not be alone in facing the challenge of improving opportunities for persistence by high-achieving minority students. Indeed, this is the first state-level study to explore the role of preparation and achievement for a cohort of students within a state. It is possible that if other states take the steps to compile longitudinal databases, they too will find serious challenges that impede the academic success of their students.

The results of the Indiana state study show that public finance policies do influence different groups in different ways. Because of their high poverty rate in the state, African Americans can benefit from the state's achievement program more than whites. Further, excessive loans can be problematic for middle-income families, who may question whether their expected earnings will grow sufficiently to justify continued borrowing. At the very least, these differences merit further and wider consideration, given the ongoing challenges facing educational opportunity for high-achieving students of color. When adequate financial aid is provided, parents' education is not the barrier for African Americans and Hispanics that it is for whites. The study findings suggest that the main challenge in providing access to college is creating engaging curriculum.

A final area of implication is that of institutional considerations. Swail, Redd, and Perna (2003) describe ten "essential factors" for establishing retention programs. Key among them are that institutions need to "rely on proven research," "support institutional research in the monitoring of programs and students," and "be sensitive to students' needs and target the most needy student populations" (pp. 116–118).

As we move into the second decade of the twenty-first century, more dramatic changes in institutional policy and practice may be needed to continue to improve student retention. Campus leaders need to remain committed to solving the problem of differential rates of persistence by underrepresented minority students. Uniting research and practice and targeting underrepresented populations with appropriate interventions will help campuses develop strong retention programs and will be the key to increasing the participation of minority students in higher education.

NEW DIRECTIONS FOR INSTITUTIONAL RESEARCH • DOI: 10.1002/ir

References

Advisory Committee on Student Financial Assistance. *Empty Promises: The Myth of College Access in America.* Washington, D.C.: Advisory Committee on Student Financial Assistance, 2002.

Allen, W. R. "The Color of Success: African-American College Student Outcomes at Predominantly White and Historically Black Public Colleges and Universities." *Harvard Educational Review,* 1992, 62(1), 26–43.

Allen, W. R., Bonous-Hammarth, M., and Suh, S. A. "Who Goes to College? High School Context, Academic Preparation, the College Choice Process, and College Attendance." In E. P. St. John (ed.), *Readings on Equal Education.* Vol. 20: *Improving Access and College Success for Diverse Students: Studies of the Gates Millennium Scholars Program.* New York: AMS Press, 2004.

Astin, A. W. *What Matters in College: Four Critical Years Revisited.* San Francisco: Jossey-Bass, 1993.

Astin, A. W., Tsui, L., and Avalos, J. *Degree Attainment Rates at American Colleges and Universities: Effects of Race, Gender, and Institutional Type.* Los Angeles: Higher Educational Research Institute, University of California, 1996.

Baker, T. L., and Vélez, W. "Access To and Opportunity in Postsecondary Education in the United States: A Review." *Sociology of Education,* 1991, Extra Issue, 82–101.

Bean, J. P. "Dropouts and Turnover: The Synthesis and Test of a Causal Model of Student Attrition." *Research in Higher Education,* 1980, 12, 155–187.

Bean, J. P., and Eaton, S. B. "A Psychological Model of College Student Retention." In J. M. Braxton (ed.), *Reworking the Student Departure Puzzle.* Nashville, Tenn.: Vanderbilt University Press, 2000.

Berger, J. B. "Optimizing Capital, Social Reproduction, and Undergraduate Persistence: A Sociological Perspective." In J. M. Braxton (ed.), *Reworking the Student Departure Puzzle.* Nashville, Tenn.: Vanderbilt University Press, 2000.

Bonous-Hammarth, M. "Value Congruence and Organizational Climates for Undergraduate Persistence." In J. C. Smart (ed.), *Higher Education: A Handbook of Theory and Research,* vol. 15. New York: Agathon Press, 2000.

Boudreau, C., and Kromrey, J. "A Longitudinal Study of Retention and Academic Performance of Participants in a Freshman Orientation Course." *Journal of College Student Development,* 1994, 35, 444–449.

Braxton, J. M. (ed.). *Reworking the Student Departure Puzzle.* Nashville, Tenn.: Vanderbilt University Press, 2000.

Braxton, J. M., Sullivan, A. S., and Johnson, R. M. "Appraising Tinto's Theory of College Student Departure." In John C. Smart (ed.), *Higher Education: Handbook of Theory and Research,* vol. 12. New York: Agathon Press, 1997.

Bynum, J. E., and Thompson, W. F. "Dropouts, Stopouts and Persisters: The Effects of Race and Sex Composition of College Classes." *College and University,* 1983, 59(1), 39–48.

Cabrera, A. F., Stampen, J. O., and Hansen, W. L. "Exploring the Effects of Ability to Pay on Persistence in College." *Review of Higher Education,* 1990, 13(3), 303–336.

Carter, D. F. "The Impact of Institutional Choice and Environments on African American and White Students' Degree Expectations." *Research in Higher Education,* 1999, 40, 17–41.

DesJardins, S. L., Ahlburg, D. A., and McCall, B. P. "A Temporal Investigation of Factors Related to Timely Degree Completion." *Journal of Higher Education,* 2002, 73(5), 555–581.

Durkheim, E. *Suicide.* (J. A. Spaulding and G. Simpson, trans.). Glencoe, Ill.: The Free Press, 1951.

Feagin, J. R., Vera, H, and Imani, N. *The Agony of Education: Black Students at White Colleges and Universities.* New York: Routledge, 1996.

Getzlaf, S. B., Sedlacek, G. M., Kearney, K. A., and Blackwell, J. M. "Two Types of Voluntary Undergraduate Attrition: Application of Tinto's Model." *Research in Higher Education,* 1984, *20*(3), 257–268.

Hanson, S. L. "Lost Talent: Unrealized Educational Aspirations and Expectations Among U.S. Youths." *Sociology of Education,* 1994, *67,* 159–183.

Hartle, T. W. "Clueless About College Costs." *Presidency,* 1998, *1*(1), 20–27.

Hatch, L. R., and Mommsen, K. "The Widening Gap in American Higher Education." *Journal of Black Studies,* 1984, *14*(4), 457–476.

Hearn, J. C. "The Relative Roles of Academic, Ascribed, and Socioeconomic Characteristics in College Destinations." *Sociology of Education,* 1984, *57,* 22–30.

Hearn, J. C. "Academic and Nonacademic Influences on the College Destinations of 1980 High School Graduates." *Sociology of Education,* 1991, *64*(July), 158–171.

"Holding a Four-Year College Degree Brings Blacks Close to Economic Parity with Whites." *Journal of Blacks in Higher Education,* 47. http://www.jbhe.com/news_views/47_four-year_collegedegrees.html. Accessed June 1, 2005.

Hurtado, S. "Linking Diversity and Educational Purpose: How Diversity Affects the Classroom Environment and Student Development." In G. Orfield (ed.), *Diversity Challenged: Evidence on the Impact of Affirmative Action.* Cambridge, Mass.: Harvard Publishing Group, 2001.

Hurtado, S., Carter, D. F., and Spuler, A. "Latino Student Transition to College: Assessing Difficulties and Factors in Successful College Adjustment." *Research in Higher Education,* 1996, *37*(2), 135–157.

Hurtado, S., Milem, J. F., Clayton-Pederson, A. R., and Allen, W. R. "Enhancing Campus Climates for Racial/Ethnic Diversity: Educational Policy and Practice." *The Review of Higher Education,* 1998, *21*(3), 279–302.

Kaltenbaugh, L. S., St. John, E. P., and Starkey, J. B. "What Difference Does Tuition Make? An Analysis of Ethnic Differences in Persistence." *Journal of Student Financial Aid,* 1999, *29*(2), 21–31.

Keller, G. "The New Demographics of Higher Education." *The Review of Higher Education,* 2001, *24*(3), 219–235.

Kuh, G. "The Other Curriculum: Out-of-Class Experiences Associated with Student Learning and Personal Development." *Journal of Higher Education,* 1995, *66,* 123–155.

Lavin, D. E., and Crook, D. B. "Open Admissions and Its Outcomes: Ethnic Differences in Long-Term Educational Attainment." *American Journal of Education,* 1990, *98*(4), 389–425.

Malveaux, J. *What's at Stake: The Social and Economic Benefits of Higher Education. Challenging Times, Clear Choices: An Action Agenda for College Access and Success.* National Dialogue on Student Financial Aid, Research Report no. 2. Washington, D.C.: Pathways to College Network, 2003.

Mehan, H., Hubbard, L., and Villanueva, I. "Forming Academic Identities: Accommodation Without Assimilation Among Involuntary Minorities." *Anthropology of Education Quarterly,* 1994, *25,* 91–117.

Myers, R. D. *College Success Programs: Executive Summary.* Washington, D.C.: Pathways to College Network, 2003.

Pascarella, E. T., Smart, J. C., and Smylie, M. A. "College Tuition Costs and Early Career Socioeconomic Achievement: Do You Get What You Pay For?" *Higher Education,* 1992, *24*(3), 275–291.

Pascarella, E. T., and Terenzini, P. T. "Predicting Freshman Persistence and Voluntary Dropout Decisions from a Theoretical Model." *Journal of Higher Education,* 1980, *51*(1), 60–75.

Pascarella, E. T., and Terenzini, P. T. *How College Affects Students: Findings and Insights from Twenty Years of Research.* San Francisco: Jossey-Bass, 1991.

Pascarella, E. T., and Terenzini, P. T. "Studying College Students in the 21st Century: Meeting New Challenges." *The Review of Higher Education*, 1998, *21*(2), 151–165.

Pathways to College Network. "A Shared Agenda: A Leadership Challenge to Improve College Access and Success." Washington, D.C.: Pathways to College Network, 2003.

Paulsen, M. B., and St. John, E. P. "Social Class and College Costs: Examining the Financial Nexus Between College Choice and Persistence." *Journal of Higher Education*, 2002, *73*(3), 189–236.

St. John, E. P. "Changes in Pricing Behavior During the 1980s: An Analysis of Selected Case Studies." *Journal of Higher Education*, 1991, *63*(2), 165–187.

St. John, E. P. *Prices, Productivity, and Investment: Assessing Financial Strategies in Higher Education*. ASHE-ERIC Higher Education Report, no. 3. Washington, D.C.: George Washington University, 1994.

St. John, E. P., Carter, D. F., Chung, C. G., and Musoba, G. D. "Diversity and Persistence in Indiana Higher Education: The Impact of Preparation, Major Choices, and Student Aid." In E. P. St. John (ed.), *Readings on Equal Education*. Vol. 21: *Public Policy and Educational Opportunity: School Reforms, Postsecondary Encouragement, and State Policies on Higher Education*. New York: AMS Press, 2006.

St. John, E. P., Paulsen, M. B., and Carter, D. F. "Diversity, College Costs, and Postsecondary Opportunity: An Examination of the College Choice-Persistence Nexus for African Americans and Whites." *Journal of Higher Education*, 2005, *76*, 545–569.

St. John, E. P., Paulsen, M. B., and Starkey, J. B. "The Nexus Between College Choice and Persistence." *Research in Higher Education*, 1996, *37*, 175–220.

Shom, C., and Spooner, S. E. "Minority Access to Higher Education: The Precollegiate Program." *NASPA Journal*, 1990, *27*(3), 222–228.

Smedley, B. D., Myers, H. F., and Harrell, S. P. "Minority-Status Stresses and the College Adjustment of Ethnic Minority Freshmen." *Journal of Higher Education*, 1993, *64*(4), 434–452.

Spady, W. G. "Dropouts from Higher Education: An Interdisciplinary Review and Synthesis." *Interchange*, 1970, *1*(1), 64–85.

Spady, W. G. "Dropouts from Higher Education: Toward an Empirical Model." *Interchange*, 1971, *2*(3), 38–62.

Stewart, D. M. "Overcoming the Barriers to Successful Participation by Minorities." *Review of Higher Education*, 1988, *11*(4), 329–335.

Swail, W. S., Redd, K. E., and Perna, L. A. *Retaining Minority Students in Higher Education: A Framework for Success*. ASHE-ERIC Higher Education Report, vol. 30, no. 2. San Francisco: Jossey-Bass, 2003.

Thomas, G. E. "The Future of Blacks in Higher Education: Recommendations and Conclusions." In G. E. Thomas (ed.), *Black Students in Higher Education: Conditions and Experiences in the 1970s*. Westport, Conn.: Greenwood Press, 1981.

Tierney, W. G. "An Anthropological Analysis of Student Participation in College." *Journal of Higher Education*, 1992, *63*(6), 603–618.

Tinto, V. "The Limits of Theory and Practice in Student Attrition." *Journal of Higher Education*, 1982, *53*, 687–700.

Tinto, V. *Leaving College: Rethinking the Causes and Cures of Student Attrition* (2nd ed.). Chicago: University of Chicago Press, 1993.

Turner, C.S.V. "Guests in Someone Else's House: Students of Color." *The Review of Higher Education*, 1994, *17*(4), 355–370.

DEBORAH FAYE CARTER is associate professor of education and director of the Center for the Study of Higher and Postsecondary Education at the University of Michigan School of Education.

NEW DIRECTIONS FOR INSTITUTIONAL RESEARCH • DOI: 10.1002/ir

4

This chapter describes how an action research framework facilitates using evaluation and assessment results to improve programs and demonstrate institutional effectiveness.

Using Action Research to Support Academic Program Improvement

Michele J. Hansen, Victor M. H. Borden

Technological innovations of the past two decades have enabled institutional researchers to collect, store, analyze, and disseminate an unprecedented quantity of program-related information. But producing more data does not necessarily guarantee that recipients will use the information effectively to develop or improve academic programs and services. Action research provides a constructive framework for ensuring that critical information is used by key stakeholders to implement data-driven interventions for continuous academic improvement. This approach allows institutional researchers to move beyond the role of data conveyor to one of facilitator of critical program and institutional change. Most important, the action research paradigm changes the relationship between the information requester and information provider from that of client and service provider to a collaborative team engaged in reflective practice and organizational learning.

Lewin and colleagues introduced action research in the 1940s as a form of experimental inquiry applied to the resolution of societal and organizational problems. World War II provided a wide array of opportunities to demonstrate how action research can be used to address social problems such as intergroup conflict, racial prejudice, and food shortages (Lewin, 1952). Early action research paradigms were also employed to link employee survey data with productivity and morale improvements in manufacturing plants (for example, Coch and French, 1948; Likert, 1967; Whyte and Hamilton, 1964).

NEW DIRECTIONS FOR INSTITUTIONAL RESEARCH, no. 130, Summer 2006 © Wiley Periodicals, Inc.
Published online in Wiley InterScience (www.interscience.wiley.com) • DOI: 10.1002/ir.179

During the postwar reconstruction years, action research moved into the education sector. McKernan (1991) reported that action research was employed as a "general strategy" for redesigning curriculum to address multifaceted social problems, such as intergroup conflicts and prejudice in the school systems (as cited in Masters, 1995). According to Masters, action research was typically conducted by outside, expert researchers in collaboration with teachers and school administrators. Stephen Corey at Teachers College at Columbia University is recognized as one of the earliest advocates of action research in the field of education. Corey "believed that the scientific method in education would bring about change because educators would be involved in both research and the application of information" (Ferrance, 2000, p. 7). However, action research had its detractors. In the mid-1950s, action research was criticized for being unscientific and the work of amateurs (McFarland and Stansell, 1993). The growing split between science and practice also detracted from the acceptance of action research. The use of scientific designs employing quantitative methodologies in laboratory settings was advocated as a more effective approach in solving educational and other social problems. But by the 1970s, the pendulum had swung back, and action research resurfaced as an effective way to bridge the gap between theory and practice (Ferrance, 2000; Masters, 1995).

The resurgence of action research in the 1970s took several forms. It was incorporated in large part in the work of Argyris and Schön (1978, 1996) on organizational learning. According to Dick (1997), action learning and action research are similar processes, as they both involve acquiring knowledge from experiences and focus on implementing interventions (actions) and reflection in a cyclical manner. Following this line of development, Senge (1990) incorporated the action research paradigm into his work, *The Fifth Discipline,* as the discipline of "mental models." The basic tenets of action research were also manifest in the growth of program evaluation research methods in both their quantitative (Rossi and Freeman, 1993; Rossi, Freeman, and Wright, 1979) and qualitative (Lincoln and Guba, 1985) forms.

The action research model has been used in more current educational and health care settings as a useful method for evaluating programs and implementing fundamental change. It has been employed as an effective approach for increasing the understanding of classroom dynamics and improving teaching and learning (Harwood, 1991), evaluating inclusive school programs (Dymond, 2001), examining the sociopolitical environment and concerns relevant for elementary school principals striving to work with disabled children and their families to implement successful inclusion programs (Brotherson, Sheriff, Milburn, and Schertz, 2001), improving a reading program for impoverished South African children (Flanagan and Nombuyiselo, 1993), and managing change in an interdisciplinary inpatient unit in a large health care organization (Barker and Barker, 1994). Thus, its employment has taken on several forms in a diversity of settings.

Harwood (1991) argues that action research can be an important tool for giving key stakeholders control at every stage of the research cycle and for advocating dialogue, reflection, and commitment to intended educational goals. Barker and Barker (1994) found the action research model to be an effective approach for reducing employee resistance to fundamental and necessary organizational changes. Their results suggested that the participatory model promoted positive staff morale, open communication, lower turnover, team problem solving, and improved goal attainment.

Colleges and universities are facing increasing demands to demonstrate that they assess the effectiveness of their programs and services and use that information to improve. As a direct result, many higher education institutions have invested significantly in building institutional research and assessment capacities. But administrators and faculty are often discouraged when they do not see these investments producing obvious improvements. We suggest in this chapter that there is a link missing in many institutional research and assessment programs and that action research facilitates the connection between evaluation research results and program improvement.

The Action Research Model

Like all forms of applied research, action research involves a process of problem identification, research question formulation, and data collection, analysis, and interpretation to determine how the results inform the research questions. As an evaluation process, the results of action research are used to develop plans for resolving the initial problem, thus "closing the loop." Action research is distinguished from other forms of applied research in the way the researcher works with other stakeholders, such as program managers, front-line staff, and organizational administrators. Within this approach, research questions are determined in discussions among stakeholders and researchers. These discussions often require several iterations so that the perspectives of differing stakeholders can be accommodated. Data collection involves both researchers and stakeholders, as does data analysis and especially interpretation of findings. Results are reviewed as part of a stakeholder action-planning activity. Planned interventions are implemented and data are collected again to evaluate the effectiveness of the interventions. The action research model is thus a cyclical, collaborative process of diagnosis, change, and evaluation.

Institutional researchers are often asked to contribute to the evaluation of campus programs and services, either directly or indirectly. Questions are posed based on real-world problems. Colleagues are consulted to refine the questions. Information is assembled, analyzed, and reported to those who posed the questions. The institutional researcher may even discuss with the client the implication of the results for decision making. However, the traditional information-support paradigm of institutional research often falls short in some notable ways from the action research approach.

NEW DIRECTIONS FOR INSTITUTIONAL RESEARCH • DOI: 10.1002/ir

For the institutional researcher, requests for information and analysis are typically viewed as independent tasks or projects rather than as a continuing cycle of planning, evaluation, and improvement. Although ostensibly some stakeholder needs will be met sufficiently following an articulate presentation of program outcomes supplemented with artful displays of graphs and charts, meaningful program improvement necessitates more explicit attempts to encourage stakeholder use of "supplied" data. The action research approach facilitates stakeholder involvement and investment in the research process.

To illustrate these differences, Table 4.1 compares the traditional institutional research approach to a specific task with the action research approach to systematic program evaluation and improvement. The comparison illustrates the ongoing and more intensive relationship between researcher and client inherent in the action research approach. The level of teamwork required by the action research approach can be intimidating or off-putting to institutional researchers and program staff alike. But before considering some of the barriers to adopting this approach, we will illustrate the model in greater detail through two examples of its application.

Applications of the Action Research Model

A comprehensive outcomes assessment program can ensure that academic support initiatives are achieving goals and are adding value to the students' educational experiences. However, as we have improved our capacity to measure a wide array of student outcomes, it has become increasingly important that we develop ways to assess why our programs and processes contribute to desirable outcomes and decrease undesirable ones. Inquiry-based evaluations provide the kinds of in-depth process information necessary to inform practice and allow for a better understanding of when and how certain interventions are effective. They can also contribute to our institutional-level efforts to effect broad-based change in strategic areas. In this section we present two concrete examples in which an action research approach was used to support academic improvement efforts and to sustain strategic planning initiatives.

Example 1: Evaluation of New Student Orientation. New Student Orientation at our institution, Indiana University-Purdue University Indianapolis (IUPUI), is designed to provide incoming students with the resources and information they need to meet university demands and acclimate to a new environment. During orientation, faculty, staff, and a student-led orientation team share the responsibility of introducing new students to the supportive and challenging learning environment on the campus. The orientation program (a full-day program) serves approximately five thousand students yearly and many of their parents (through a Family Connections Program).

**Table 4.1. Action Research Contrasted with the Traditional
Institutional Research Approach**

	Action Research Approach	Traditional Institutional Research Approach
Research Question and Evaluation Focus	The evaluation focus is developed together among the researchers and stakeholders (information requesters). The questions and focus are often deferred until appropriate vested parties are brought together as a team to consider the issues and possible spheres of influence that the research results can affect.	The research question or request is presented to the researchers either as a top-down directive or a bottom-up request. There is typically some discussion to clarify the question and the context for use.
Data Collection	The stakeholders often have some role in collecting data or in working with the researchers to understand nuances of available information. The responsibility for the integrity of the data is shared.	The researchers are responsible for finding available data and collecting new information where needed. The researchers are ultimately held accountable for the integrity of the information.
Data Analysis and Interpretation	The researchers involve stakeholders in all stages of data analysis. Preliminary results are presented and discussed. Further analyses are shaped by those discussions.	The researchers are often entirely responsible up through dissemination. They may consult with stakeholders to gain insight into the results.
Report Presentation and Dissemination	The presentation and report writing responsibilities are shared by researcher and stake-holder representatives. Presentations involve more discussion compared to traditional approach. The process of information sharing is more dynamic and iterative.	The researchers often prepare formal, static reports and present results to stakeholders.
Follow-up	Key stakeholders design an action plan based on results. Data collection is included in the follow-up plan so that actions can be monitored and evaluated for effectiveness. Further lines of inquiry are established for the next cycle of research.	Stakeholders may request some additional analyses, or clarification may be needed based on reported information. This often is the end of the process.

A comprehensive evaluation of the program was requested by a faculty governance committee to determine if the orientation program was achieving its intended educational outcomes for incoming students. Generally, the evaluation was designed to help provide an informed perspective on the major strengths and deficiencies of the orientation program to derive data-driven program improvements.

Research Question and Evaluation Focus. During the initial phases of the evaluation process, orientation leaders and planners were brought together to define clearly the desired outcomes of the evaluation process. A collective decision was made to focus the evaluation on reevaluating the goals of orientation, determining if the diverse needs of new students (including commuters, international students, students from underrepresented ethnic groups, and older students) were being met and to assess the extent to which orientation was affecting new students' knowledge levels, attitudes, and behaviors. Active involvement of the multiple stakeholders involved in implementing orientation (orientation leaders, faculty, administrators, student affairs staff, and student peer mentors) was critical for defining manageable goals that had direct implications for potential programmatic changes. Moreover, it was also vital to seek input from a large sample of incoming student orientation participants.

Data Collection. Quantitative and qualitative techniques were employed to obtain a comprehensive understanding of the impact of New Student Orientation on student participants. A series of fourteen focus groups was conducted in spring and fall 2002. The focus groups were designed to seek input from faculty, students, advisors, administrators, and student affairs staff, as they are critical stakeholders in the orientation program. In addition, a questionnaire was administered to first-year student orientation participants enrolled in First-Year Seminar courses during the fall 2002 semester to assess their perceptions of New Student Orientation. The questionnaire was designed to measure students' self-reported changes in behaviors, learning gains, and perceptions of orientation three months after the start of the fall semester. At that point, students could report how orientation helped them in making their transition to IUPUI.

Orientation leaders were actively involved in designing the focus group protocol and the self-administered questionnaire. Seeking their involvement ensured that the instruments were designed to assess useful information and ideally served to increase the chances that the collected data would be used to guide program improvements.

Data Reporting and Feedback. The orientation leaders were involved in the initial stages of data analysis. Preliminary results were presented and discussed in a meeting with the Director of New Student Orientation, the Assistant Director of New Student Orientation, and the Assistant Dean of University College, the unit that houses all the orientation programs. The data feedback session included a written report and verbal discussions of key findings. The information was provided to inform the orientation leaders about the perceptions concerning the current state of the orientation program and encouraged their involvement in implementing potential changes. The orientation leaders asserted that commitment on behalf of the campus community was essential for change to be initiated and sustained; so, following the feedback meeting and suggested report revisions, the written report was distributed to key faculty committees and other relevant campus groups. The written report was also distributed to all focus group participants.

Development of Action Plans. Findings were presented to orientation leaders and other key stakeholder groups in a way that facilitated dialogue, conversation, and the development of action plans. For instance, the recommendations were framed as questions to guide the action planning process. The following is an excerpt from the New Student Orientation Program Evaluation Report (Hansen and Lowenkron, 2003):

> We recommend that New Student Orientation planners use this report to develop data-driven action plans to improve the orientation process. The following questions could serve as a starting point to guide action planning:
>
> Are the above goals the most appropriate ones for New Student Orientation at IUPUI?
> Would it be beneficial for orientation planners to take a strategic planning approach and engage in a self-reflective process in which they identify an agreed-upon vision, mission, and the specific goals of orientation?
> What implementation procedures could be introduced to create a more efficient orientation (e.g., less wait-time, reduced feelings of information overload, and a more organized experience)?
> What strategies could be employed to make orientation a more interactive, engaging process so that students make more meaningful connections with other students, faculty, advisors, and student affairs staff? (p. 4)

Action plans were developed to deal with the patterns found in the data, as prioritized by the orientation leaders. For example, evaluation results suggested that new students were not making sustained connections with other students, faculty, advisors, or student affairs staff during orientation. New Student Orientation planners decided to start the orientation program by having new students form small groups rather than beginning the day by having students listen to a large, lecture hall presentation. Other survey responses included complaints about long wait-times, information overload, and lack of organization; the data-driven action plans therefore included developing strategies to expand the campus tour; providing a more in-depth, interactive technology session; and implementing a more efficient process with more clearly defined goals; employing more intentional efforts to help new students make more sustained contacts and connections with the campus community during orientation; including more information about costs of attending and financial aid; and providing more extensive, meaningful advising sessions.

Implementation. Based on the dialogue surrounding the findings of the initial evaluation, orientation leaders implemented a series of program changes during the fall 2003 orientation program, such as moving the campus tour to the morning to provide students with a better sense of direction for the day; increasing the amount of interaction the students have with peers, university faculty, and staff during the program; creating a new student life program called Freshman Year in a Flash (designed to be a simulation activity of the student's first year); implementing a new group advising model; and developing a theoretical underpinning for the program based on academic integration, social integration, and self-efficacy (Hansen, Lowenkron, Engler, and Evenbeck, 2004).

Assessment. Once the action plans were initiated, further information was gathered to determine if the proposed changes had been implemented as conceptualized and were perceived positively by students and if further modifications in the plans were necessary. Orientation leaders and the researchers developed an orientation "exit instrument" (completed by students during the program) to monitor the impacts of these changes. Moreover, the questionnaire designed to assess student participants' perceptions three months after the start of the fall semester was re-administered to determine the impacts of the changes employed during the summer 2003 series of orientation programs. It is notable that the exact instrument was administered in an effort to assess changes in students' perceptions of the program. Results from the fall 2003 survey administration suggested that the program modifications were particularly effective in the following areas (based on significant findings from independent sample t-tests): providing opportunities for students to make meaningful connections with other students and faculty, providing effective advising sessions, creating feelings of pride in the institution, informing students about campus life (campus-sponsored events and activities), and providing students with information about critical academic supports (for example, the Math Assistance Center). Orientation leaders and researchers have continued to work toward data collection efforts to monitor program effectiveness and provide information on how orientation is meeting the academic needs of our diverse student body (for example, transfer students, students over the age of twenty-five, and ethnic minorities). Thus, the evaluation of the orientation program has become an ongoing, reflective, cyclical process.

Example 2: Improving the Campus Climate for Diversity. The IUPUI Chancellor's Diversity Cabinet was established in January 1999 "to oversee the ultimate transformation of IUPUI from a campus that believes in diversity to a campus that lives its commitment to diversity" (Bepko, 2000). In its first year, the cabinet took stock of the campus climate for diversity by conducting a self-study under the guidance of a nationally renowned expert. As part of this process, the cabinet invited to its meetings representatives from the various academic schools and administrative areas to learn about initiatives under way in each unit to promote diversity as an organizational and academic asset.

By the end of that first year, the cabinet developed a vision for diversity at IUPUI that includes the following working definition of diversity for the campus:

"At Indiana University Purdue University Indianapolis (IUPUI), diversity means three things: (1) diversity is an educational and social asset to be reflected in our learning and work objectives, (2) the persons who comprise our academic community reflect both the current diversity of our service region as well as the evolving demographics of a state and city that aspire to participate fully in a global society, and (3) IUPUI's social and physical environment will enable all of its members to succeed to the fullest extent of their potential." (http://www.iupui.edu/diversity/vision.html).

The Vision for Diversity also included thirteen concrete performance objectives that require significant participation from virtually all academic and administrative units. In the fall of 2002, the chancellor asked the staff of the Office of Information Management and Institutional Research (IMIR) to develop a set of diversity indicators that would provide a "score card" regarding campus progress toward obtaining the concrete objectives and broader goals stated in the vision.

Research Question and Evaluation Focus. Rather than proceeding directly as requested, IMIR staff requested a meeting with the cabinet to discuss how this request for a summative evaluation could be transformed into a more formative process. During this meeting, a sequence of steps was described wherein two steering groups would be formed to guide the process. One group—the technical measurement group—would bring together individuals with expertise and experience in conceptualizing and measuring diversity. This group's task would be to work from the Vision for Diversity to develop a manageable number of general performance objectives that represented the breadth of the vision. The product of this group would be sent to an administrative group that included individuals from academic and administrative units that would "do something" to improve the campus climate for diversity. The second group's objective would be to provide a reality check on the measures produced by the first group. That is, they would provide feedback regarding the likelihood that the programs and activities currently focusing on improving the campus climate for diversity would result in positive changes in the measures developed by the first group.

Through an iterative series of meetings, the groups worked their way through the general indicators and then down to a set of specific measures. Staff from the IMIR office participated in both sets of meetings to help integrate the process and to provide information regarding the current and potential availability of the data to develop pertinent measures. The process resulted in the articulation of eight broad performance objectives, each of which was supported by three to five concrete measures (the complete set can be seen at http://iport.iupui.edu/performance/perf_diversity.htm).

Data Collection. The information needed for the diversity performance indicators derived from a range of sources. For expediency's sake, the first iteration included measures that were already available in a centrally collected form (for example, institutional databases and campuswide surveys of students, faculty, and staff).

Data Reporting and Feedback. The available measures were assembled for review by the Chancellor's Diversity Cabinet. Cabinet members were asked to rate each indicator using the following scale:

Green: Either at an acceptable level or clearly heading in the right direction and not requiring any immediate change in course of action. Continuing support should be provided to sustain momentum in these areas.
Yellow: Not at an acceptable level; either improving, but not as quickly as desired, or declining slightly. Strategies and approaches should be reviewed and appropriate adjustments taken to reach an acceptable level or desired rate of improvement.
Red: The current status or direction of change is unacceptable. Immediate, high-priority actions should be taken to address this area.

Initial ratings were collected through an electronic survey. The results were tabulated and served as a starting point in a face-to-face meeting for developing consensus on the judgments. Little or no discussion was solicited over the few items for which there was unanimous (or close to unanimous) initial ratings. For indicators that had substantial variation in judgments, advocates for each rating presented their logic and, after a modest period of discussion, another vote was taken. For two indicators, further information was requested before final votes were taken. Ultimately, each indicator received at least a three-quarter majority vote for its final rating. The final ratings were included in the campus performance indicator Web site (referenced above), as well as in the chancellor's annual State of Diversity address (see, for example, http://www.iupui.edu/administration/chancellorsnews/state_of_diversity_04.pdf).

Development of Action Plans. The agenda for the first post-rating meeting of the Chancellor's Diversity Cabinet focused on the development of action plans for addressing the results of the rating process. The resultant plan had three general components:

1. A set of actions to address the one "red" evaluation—retention and graduation of a diverse student body.
2. A review of activities in place to foster progress of the other indicator areas to identify any gaps.

3. A plan for obtaining more pertinent data to improve the measures associated with some of the indicators.

Action. In response to the high priority given to the retention-graduation indicator, the cabinet commissioned the IMIR office to develop a report focusing on retention and graduation rate gaps at the school and major program level. Resources were provided to ensure that the report was conducted in a timely manner so that the results were available to the deans of the academic schools in the middle of the spring semester. The report (available at http://www.imir.iupui.edu/infore/mi/Spring03/SGRR03.asp) received considerable attention and was followed by requests for local presentation at several schools, as well as follow-up information requests to probe into certain findings. In addition, several measures included in the report will now be monitored annually as part of the indicator report.

A second action was the convening of the inaugural IUPUI Excellence in Diversity Conference, during which the indicators were used as a launching point for focusing program-specific efforts on the broader campus goals. A third line of action involved the convening of a working group to review and revise the items related to campus climate for diversity included in the campuswide surveys of students, faculty, and staff.

Assessment. The Chancellor's Diversity Cabinet continues to monitor implementation of actions taken in response to the first iteration of the diversity-indicator process. The diversity indicators have been updated and reviewed each year since their inception and priorities for the current year have been adjusted to reflect any changes.

Whereas the first example (the New Student Orientation Program) focused on a specific program, this example relates to a higher-level set of processes. As such, it provides insight into how the action research process can affect the domain of executive management. Within this domain, the connections between action and research are more diffuse and less direct. As a result, the action research process becomes more akin to a brokering process for facilitating organizational development and transformation (as noted by Jackson, 2003).

Possible Barriers to the Action Research Approach

Action research requires the researchers to act as facilitators and become more intimately involved in program and unit processes as they seek a greater understanding of the subject of evaluation. At the same time, program staff need to develop a research orientation as they participate actively in making decisions about research questions, methodology, instrumentation, analysis, and deployment. As they assume these roles, both parties may experience role stress in the forms of role ambiguity, role conflict, and role overload.

Role ambiguity results when individuals do not have clear information regarding their job expectations and when there is lack of clarity concerning job tasks, role function, and rewards (Rizzo, House, and Lirtzman, 1970). Role conflict results when simultaneous roles require conflicting actions. For example, a researcher may feel her role in designing and reporting on a valid instrument to measure program outcomes may be in direct conflict with the motivation of a program administrator to deliver good news to the campus community about the program's outcomes. Role overload occurs when there is a perception that too many tasks are required and there is insufficient time to fulfill job requirements. In addition to having to fulfill daily job demands, during the action research process, program administrators and institutional researchers may be given supplemental responsibilities. For example, program administrators may be asked to help design assessment instruments and researchers may have to attend unit or program administration meetings during the multiple stages of the action research model.

Adverse reactions among action research participants to ambiguous responsibilities, increased work demands, and role conflicts can serve as barriers to implementing effective action research strategies as participants experience stress and feel less committed to the tasks associated with active participation. Thus, the successful implementation of action research necessitates that decisive steps be taken to help minimize the potential occurrence of these adverse reactions.

Seo (2003) describes three barriers that can inhibit the action research approach and thereby limit learning and change: emotional barriers, political obstacles, and managerial control imperatives. Seo argues that it is critical to focus on removing emotional barriers to achieve change in underlying values and assumptions, which is essential to effect change. Political coalitions can become barriers to translating individual and group learning into organizational-level learning and change unless the individual actors "both understand the underlying political dynamics within the organization and have adequate strategies to overcome them" (Seo, 2003, p. 12). Seo also argues that learning may not contribute to fundamental behavioral and organizational change because the larger socioeconomic system shapes organizational functioning and may exert enormous pressure and control over managers.

Overcoming Barriers to Implementing the Action Research Approach

To implement the action research method effectively, decisive efforts must be exerted to overcome these barriers to participants' learning and programmatic change. Role ambiguity may be minimized by beginning the process with clear descriptions of role expectations, duties, and potential rewards. In addition, establishing an atmosphere of trust and ongoing open communication can decrease participants' feelings of uncertainty. An open communication strategy, coupled with clear and consistent task guidelines, can reduce feelings of role conflict. In order to reduce feelings of role overload, it is important that participants be informed up front about the demands so they can begin to plan for the level of commitment essential for a successful process. It may also be helpful to provide participants with a cost-benefit analysis regarding the action research model, describing that such an effort may require more time, energy, and commitment, but that it may ultimately result in fundamental and sustained program improvements and even long-term fiscal benefits.

Seo (2003) recommends three ways to overcome each of his proposed barriers: "up-building" positive affect, leveraging opposing forces, and bringing external legitimacy to the organization. In up-building positive affect, Seo advocates for starting with a relatively superficial win-win approach prior to engaging in the more probing efforts to uncover and change problematic assumptions and beliefs. Overcoming political obstacles requires the participants to understand and use political dynamics in their discussions and actions. Seo also suggests that external consultants can be used to overcome managerial control imperatives by illuminating external reality and providing a legitimate impetus for new directions.

Applying Action Research to Higher Education Reform

In addition to the continuous pressure to improve academic programs in an effort to respond to the accountability demands of external and internal stakeholders, there is also a momentum to launch changes in higher education settings that are more wide ranging. On the basis of a strategic planning process undertaken with participants from the Association of American Colleges and Universities (AAC&U), Schneider and Shoenberg (1998) contend that higher education is in an era of transformative change. These authors report that college and university leaders are committed to making fundamental changes in an effort to improve teaching and learning. External demands are creating a situation in which institutions must implement critical changes to remain competitive and effective providers of educational services. Institutions that are able to implement fundamental change successfully will thrive and survive in the next decade, but such change often comes at a price. When change is introduced into a system, staff members, faculty, and students may feel that their stable and predictable world is being replaced with one that is unpredictable and uncertain.

Past research has shown that changing work environments can result in employees experiencing increased levels of uncertainty and role ambiguity (see, for example, Ashford, 1988; Bennett, Lehman, and Forst, 1999; Saifer, 1996). According to Morris (1992), the limited human capacity to accept change may constrain organizational responses to environmental demands and thus may impede the success of organizational transitions. In fact, successful program and institutional change necessitates the acceptance of proposed interventions as well as the maintenance of sustained support for the changes (Carr, 1997; Lewin, 1952).

Many of the proposed strategies for promoting support for change focus on involving employees in the change process. Kotter and Schlesinger (1992) suggest that involving key stakeholders in the change process and encouraging input are likely to foster commitment to proposed changes. The participatory nature of action research makes it a valuable method for successfully implementing change in a variety of educational settings.

According to Schuh and Upcraft (2001), one of the primary criteria for accreditation in higher education is the ability to demonstrate that assessment results have been used continuously to improve institutional effectiveness. They report that accreditation depends on the institution's capacity to raise critical questions about program efficacy, identify appropriate answers, and improve processes in the light of assessment findings. The action research model is a useful tool for promoting the collaboration, dialogue, and collective analysis required among faculty, administration, and governing boards for achieving high standards of educational excellence.

Conclusions and Implications

Action research offers an alternative to traditional applied research or information-support models that currently guide institutional research. The cyclical and participatory processes associated with action research are effective mechanisms for facilitating fundamental organizational change and for linking program evaluation results with ongoing improvements.

The action research model changes the relationship between researcher and program administrator, introducing a higher level of collaboration, with both parties taking on responsibilities for each other's work more than they might in a more traditional model. The relationship may be uncomfortable for researchers who seek to remain removed from the roles and responsibilities of the administrator. Similarly, it may be uncomfortable for the program administrator who does not want to be bothered with the technical and methodological details of research. This level of discomfort is directly related to resistance to change, which is what action research is all about. Potential barriers to implementing effective action research—such as role ambiguity, role conflict, and political barriers—can be overcome if recognized and intentionally managed.

The action research paradigm has a variety of practical implications, as it provides a useful framework for planning and implementing successful participatory program evaluations. Effective change-management programs and, on a broader scope, institutional transformations necessitate key stakeholder participation and support. The interaction, dialogue, and collective critical inquiry fostered via the action research process is likely to result in genuine commitment and support for essential academic program and institutional changes.

References

Argyris, C., and Schön, D. A. *Organizational Learning: A Theory of Action Perspective.* Reading, Mass.: Addison-Wesley, 1978.

Argyris, C., and Schön, D. A. *Organizational Learning II: Theory, Method, and Practice.* Reading, Mass.: Addison-Wesley, 1996.

Ashford, S. J. "Individual Strategies for Coping with Stress During Organizational Transitions." *The Journal of Applied Behavioral Science,* 1988, *24,* 19–36.

Barker, S. B., and Barker, R. T. "Managing Change in an Interdisciplinary Inpatient Unit: An Action Research Approach." *Journal of Mental Health Administration,* 1994, *21*(1), 80–92.

Bennett, J. B., Lehman, W. E., and Forst, J. K. "Change, Transfer Climate, and Customer Orientation: A Contextual Model and Analysis of Change-Driven Training." *Group and Organization Management,* 1999, *24*(2), 188–216.

Bepko, G. Chancellor's "Call to Action." 2000. http://www.iupui.edu/diversity/cabinet. html. Accessed May 21, 2005.

Brotherson, M. J., Sheriff, G., Milburn, P., and Schertz, M. "Elementary School Principals and Their Needs and Issues for Inclusive Early Childhood Programs." *Topics in Early Childhood Education,* 2001, *21,* 31–46.

Carr, A. "The Learning Organization: New Lessons/Thinking for the Management of Change and Management Development." *Journal of Management Development,* 1997, *16,* 224–232.

Coch, L., and French, J. R. "Overcoming Resistance to Change." *Human Relations,* 1948, *1,* 512–532.

Dick, B. "Action Learning and Action Research, 1997." http://www.scu.edu.au/schools/ gcm/ar/arp/actlearn.html. Accessed Mar. 21, 2006.

Dymond, S. K. "A Participatory Action Research Approach to Evaluating Inclusive School Programs." *Focus on Autism and Other Developmental Disabilities,* 2001, *16,* 54–64.

Ferrance, E. "Themes in Education: Action Research. Northeast and Islands Regional Educational Laboratory at Brown University. A program of the Educational Alliance, 2000." http://www.lab.brown.edu/public/pubs/themes_ed/act_research.pdf. Accessed Mar. 21, 2006.

Flanagan, W., and Nombuyiselo, M. "Understanding and Learning: One Teacher's Story." *Cambridge Journal of Education,* 1993, *23*(1), 33–41.

Hansen, M. J., and Lowenkron, A. "New Student Orientation Program Evaluation Report." Unpublished report. Indianapolis: Indiana University-Purdue University Indianapolis, 2003.

Hansen, M. J., Lowenkron, A. H., Engler, A. C., and Evenbeck, S. E. "An Action Research Approach to Evaluating New Student Orientation." Paper presented at the annual meeting of the Association for Institutional Research, Boston, Mass., 2004.

Harwood, D. "Action Research Versus Interaction Analysis: A Time for Reconciliation? A Reply to Barry Hutchinson." *British Educational Research Journal,* 1991, *17*(1), 67–73.

Jackson, N. (ed.). *Engaging and Changing Higher Education through Brokerage.* Aldershot, England: Ashgate, 2003.

Kotter, J. P., and Schlesinger, L. A. "Choosing Strategies for Change." In J. J. Gabarro (ed.), *Managing People and Organizations.* Boston: Harvard Business School, 1992.

Lewin, K. *Field Theory in Social Science.* London: Tavistock, 1952.

Likert, R. *The Human Organization.* New York: McGraw Hill, 1967.

Lincoln, Y. S., and Guba, E. G. *Naturalistic Inquiry*. Thousand Oaks, Calif.: Sage, 1985.

Masters, J. "The History of Action Research." In I. Hughes (ed.), *Action Research Electronic Reader,* 1995. http://www.behs.cchs.usyd.edu.au/arow/Reader/rmasters.htm. Accessed May 10, 2005.

McFarland, K. P., and Stansell, J. C. "Historical Perspectives." In L. Patterson, S. M. Santa, C. G. Short, and K. Smith (eds.), *Teachers Are Researchers: Reflection and Action.* Newark, Del.: International Reading Association, 1993.

McKernan, J. *Curriculum Action Research: A Handbook of Methods and Resources for the Reflective Practitioner.* London: Kogan Page, 1991.

Morris, L. "Resistance to Change." *Training and Development,* 1992, *46,* 74–77.

Rizzo, J. R., House, R. J., and Lirtzman, S. I. "Role Conflict and Ambiguity in Complex Organizations." *Administrative Science Quarterly,* 1970, *15,* 150–163.

Rossi, P. H., and Freeman, H. E. *Evaluation: A Systematic Approach* (6th ed.). London: Sage, 1993.

Rossi, P. H., Freeman, H. E., and Wright, S. *Evaluation: A Systematic Approach.* Thousand Oaks, Calif.: Sage, 1979.

Saifer, A. G. "Organizational Change, Stress and Job Satisfaction: An Empirically Derived Model." Dissertation Abstracts International, 57–04B. AAG9625612, 1996.

Schneider, C. G., and Shoenberg, R. *Contemporary Understandings of Liberal Education: The Academy in Transition.* Washington, D.C.: Association of American Colleges and Universities, 1998.

Schuh, J. H., and Upcraft, M. L. *Assessment Practice in Student Affairs: An Applications Manual.* San Francisco: Jossey-Bass, 2001.

Senge, P. M. *The Fifth Discipline: The Art and Practice of a Learning Organization.* New York: Doubleday, 1990.

Seo, M. G. "Overcoming Emotional Barriers, Political Obstacles, and Control Imperatives in the Action-Science Approach to Individual and Organizational Learning." *Academy of Management: Learning and Education,* 2003, *2*(1), 7–21.

Whyte, W., and Hamilton, E. *Action Research for Management.* Homewood, Ill.: Irwin-Dorsey, 1964.

MICHELE J. HANSEN *is director of assessment for University College at Indiana University-Purdue University Indianapolis (IUPUI).*

VICTOR M. H. BORDEN *is associate vice chancellor for information management and institutional research and associate professor of psychology at Indiana University-Purdue University Indianapolis (IUPUI).*

5

Action research involves researchers and practitioners in collaborative projects and provides a means of integrating evaluation into the reform process.

Using Action Inquiry to Address Critical Challenges

Edward P. St. John, Jeffrey S. McKinney, Tina Tuttle

Strategies for using research as a basis for organizational reform in higher education have evolved over the past half-century, from total systems approaches to complex strategies that combine central and decentralized action. To put in context the inquiry process used in the Indiana Project on Academic Success (IPAS), this chapter first reconsiders the history of organizational reform efforts in higher education. Next, the inquiry approach itself is described, followed by a summary of the current status of the IPAS project and a few examples of the ways campuses have responded to this process approach to change.

Situating Action Inquiry

Using research to inform large-scale systemic approaches to change in higher education first gained momentum in the master planning movement of the 1960s (Halstead, 1974). Planning, budgeting, and evaluation systems were among the early attempts to organize universities using research and evaluation as an integral part of the change process (Weathersby and Balderston, 1972), an approach that evolved from the Allied war effort in World War II. Modern management methods, including operations research, were

Note: The project described in this chapter was funded by Lumina Foundation for Education. The opinions expressed in this chapter are the authors' and do not necessarily reflect policies or positions of the foundation.

introduced into universities in the early 1970s (Balderston, 1974), largely in response to budgetary problems. These methods alleviated some of the financial tension of the period (Balderston, 1974; Cheit, 1974) but did not noticeably change academic or student affairs programs.

In fact, formal systems approaches often did not work well in higher education, given the decentralized nature of academic governance. In the early 1980s, a variety of strategic planning approaches emerged as a means of assessing context, envisioning new forms of action, and reorganizing academic units and programs (Chaffee, 1983; Keller, 1983; Norris and Poulton, 1987). For more than two decades, strategic methods for organizing and guiding the change process have been widely used in higher education. However, systematic evaluative research has not kept up with the changes on the planning side of the enterprise.

There is, of course, a long history of assessment methods (for example, Banta, Rudolph, Van Dyke, and Fisher, 1996), but these methods, too, have focused on the front end of change, responding to accountability systems and funding criteria. However, the evolution of these methods has not generated many evaluations of the reform efforts. It is possible that the adaptive change model that has evolved in higher education—using strategic methods to scan research to inform adaptive changes—works to address many of the challenges that come up. These adaptive and strategic change processes can be quicker than inquiry-based approaches because evaluation takes time.

Efforts to improve retention have also implicitly used this strategic approach. Interventions have evolved based on an understanding of the research, but evaluations of those interventions are rare (as discussed in Chapters One and Two of this volume). This situation is a reflection of the strategic orientation, looking at research as part of the initial phase of change and adapting organizationally. However, leaving evaluation out of the change process inhibits learning and adaptation.

While strategic action may be appropriate for mission-oriented planning and for adaptive changes, it may not be the best approach to solving the most serious problems. Habermas (1984, 1987, 1991) distinguishes between two forms of action: strategic and communicative. Strategic action focuses on achieving goals; communicative action aims to build understanding. When there are recurrent problems with causes that are not readily apparent, we need to build an understanding of underlying causes before charging uncritically ahead with solutions that may not fit the problem. In higher education, not searching for causes is particularly problematic because most of the research is based on traditional-age students and traditional institutions. However, the most critical challenges often involve addressing the educational needs of nontraditional populations, like work students. Identifying strategies for improving opportunity for students who do not fit the traditional profile may require stepping off well-traveled paths.

There are critical challenges that have lingered unresolved at most campuses. Frequently, these challenges include issues related to diversity and the needs of new entrants. As Carter's review in Chapter Three of this volume illustrates, the efforts to improve opportunity for students of color have focused on student engagement and orientation. We would expect this to be so, given the research emphasis on engagement. However, analyses of persistence by students of color in Indiana, at least, revealed serious problems within academic fields. In a study of the Indiana cohort who graduated from public high schools in 2000 and enrolled in Indiana colleges the next academic year, St. John, Carter, Chung, and Musoba (2006) examined the impact of academic preparation, student aid, and college academic experience on persistence in college by African Americans, Hispanics, and whites and reached the following conclusion:

> There were substantial differences in the association between major choices and persistence across the three groups. For whites and Hispanics a few majors were positively associated with persistence. However, for African Americans, several academic majors were negatively associated with persistence and there were no positive associations. These findings raise questions about engagement in academic programs and whether the content of major programs meets the expectations of African Americans. Since these analyses control for preparation and achievement, it simply is not possible or appropriate to reduce these findings to ability or preparation differences. Instead, these findings point to serious academic problems in Indiana higher education. Faculties in health, business, education, and computer science in particular need to consider why their majors do not support persistence by diverse students. (pp. 377–378)

Until the academic community digs beneath the surface of these challenges, it won't be possible to know whether the problem is prejudice or just a failure to generate new knowledge and to act in new ways. Pondering this situation in Indiana, the possibility of latent prejudice lingers, especially as long as faculty fail to consider options. St. John and colleagues continue, "This atmosphere of unintended discrimination may exist in Indiana higher education. The fact that, controlling for preparation, college grades, and remedial courses, African Americans in several applied majors—business, education, health, and computer science—do not persist as well as their peers with undeclared majors reveals a serious problem with the engagement of the best and the brightest minority students. The causes cannot be cast off on the lack of parental education or low achievement. The challenge resides within the colleges and universities in the state." (p. 380)

This issue in Indiana illustrates that these challenges can linger indefinitely as long as colleges and universities do not take them seriously. Historically black colleges can be looked to as models for new academic strategies that are more supportive of African Americans (for example, Allen, Epps, and Haniff, 1991; Thomas, 1985), but it also seems critical to begin to build better evaluative information on reform efforts in traditionally white institutions responding to the challenges of serving new clientele.

The inquiry process had been previously proposed (St. John, 1994, 1995, 2003) as an approach that could be used to address critical challenges in higher education. The inquiry process involved building an understanding of the challenge, looking internally and externally for possible solutions, evaluating options, developing action plans, implementing plans as pilot tests, and evaluating results, then reengaging in understanding the challenges based on this experience (using a learning cycle). An argument was that some problems required exploration as to why a challenge existed in the first place, before beginning the process of looking externally at research and practice. An adaptation of this approach was proposed for faculty (Paulsen and St. John, 2002) as a means of improving faculty engagement in research on teaching and retention and for linking educational improvement with internal resource acquisition within universities that had incentive budgeting systems.

These arguments informed the initial model for IPAS, which was designed to start with research on persistence and to engage campuses in inquiry that addressed critical challenges they identified. Thus, the IPAS project represents an opportunity to learn about a new approach to organizational change, one that focuses on the most critical challenges.

Introducing Action Inquiry

The action inquiry process used in the IPAS project started with assessments using statewide data systems to identify statewide and campus-level challenges. Fifteen Indiana campuses were initially involved—seven campuses of Indiana University, four community college campuses, a regional campus of the Purdue University system, two state universities, a public two-year campus, and two private colleges. Teams from each of the campuses attended the initial meeting, but participation became a problem: the project would have required extra time from professional staff whose time was heavily committed.

Initially, the statewide assessment started with the 2000 cohort, examining preparation, college choices, and persistence. We had assumed that the transitions between high school and college would be a major concern in the project, given the emphasis on changes in high school preparation in the state. These analyses were not well received by many of the campuses for a couple of reasons: the analyses were not easy to understand even by people who had a background in statistics, and many of the campuses were more concerned about nontraditional-age students than the college-age cohort. The project team adapted, generating more studies and spending more time explaining them to campus teams. In addition, efforts were made to introduce the assessment and inquiry process. By the end of the assessment process, it had become clear that the state system was facing two major challenges: ensuring equal opportunity for students of color and enabling continuing enrollment by the burgeoning number of working students in the state.

New Directions for Institutional Research • DOI: 10.1002/ir

The training provided workshops to introduce the inquiry process, summarized in the following steps:

1. *Build an Understanding of the Challenge.* Consider why the challenge exists. What solutions have been tried in the past, and how well did they work? What aspects of the challenge have not been adequately addressed? What aspects of the challenge require more study? Develop hypotheses about the causes for the challenges using data to test the hypotheses. Do the explanations hold up to the evidence? What more preparation might help students in your major programs?

2. *Look Internally and Externally for Solutions.* Talk with people on campus about how they have addressed related challenges. Consider best practices for retention and how they might be adapted to meet local needs. Visit other campuses that have tried out different approaches to the problem. How well would these alternatives address the challenge at your campus?

3. *Assess Possible Solutions.* Consider alternatives in relation to the understanding of the problem developed in Step 1. Will the solutions address the challenge at your campus? How can the solution be pilot tested? If you tried out the solution, how would you know if it worked? What information would you need to know how well it worked?

4. *Develop Action Plans.* Action plans should address the implementation of solutions that should be pilot tested. Consider solutions that can be implemented by current staff. If there are additional costs, develop budgets for consideration internally and externally. (Remember, seeking additional funds can slow down the change process.) Develop action plans with time frames for implementation and evaluation.

5. *Implement Pilot Test and Evaluate.* Provide feedback to workgroups and campus coordinating team. Use evaluation results to refine the solution. Also, evaluation can be used as a basis for seeking additional funding from internal and external sources, if needed.

The workshops focused on the first two steps of the process. After the workshops, students and staff working on the IPAS project conducted literature reviews to assist with the process of looking externally for solutions. In a few instances, campus teams made site visits to other campuses. In addition, external project advisors were brought to Indiana to provide workshops on topics that appeared to be of interest to all campuses, including working students, faculty inquiry, minority student persistence in scientific fields, and transfer and articulation.

The campus-level view of the inquiry process is presented in Figure 5.1. Campuses were encouraged to review state analyses in comparison to the campus-level studies they were provided. During the first year, statewide meetings were conducted on minority retention, transfer and articulation, and organizing the inquiry process. Participation at these

Figure 5.1. IPAS Campus Inquiry Model

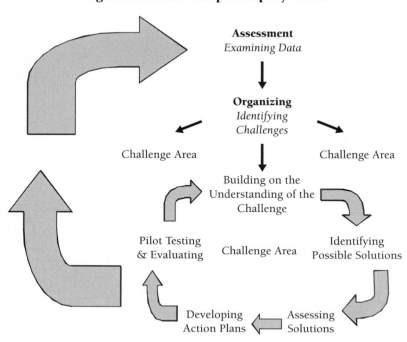

meetings was variable, but a group of interested people emerged at about half of the campuses.

Not all campuses attended regional training, nor did all campuses actively engage in the IPAS process. One private college dropped out before the training on inquiry. They already had a few large, funded projects, and because this one did not include funding they did not want to proceed. After participating in the second round of training, the two state universities and one of the public two-year campuses dropped out and did not participate in subsequent sessions. We expect that the labor-intensive nature of the change process, inconsistent technical support, and lack of resources were reasons for disengaging. (During the first year, the project had the equivalent of two and a half professional staff and one and a half graduate assistants. The project team relied on student volunteers to provide technical support in some instances. The process took more time than either student volunteers or some campus participants could manage.) College administrators and faculty often expect external funding for participation in projects, and involvement in unfunded projects requires volunteers. The main campus of the IU system and two regional campuses lacked any consistent involvement. While our original design called for more extensive involvement of campuses, a more sporadic model of engagement evolved.

NEW DIRECTIONS FOR INSTITUTIONAL RESEARCH • DOI: 10.1002/ir

In spite of these obstacles, nine out of sixteen campuses have participated in the process, developing one or more active workgroups engaged in
inquiry, as shown in Table 5.1. In each of these groups, teams have been
involved in using action inquiry to address challenges they identified. The
research we conducted provided their baseline information, but the challenges reflect their concerns. Although the extent of involvement was less
than originally envisioned, we knew going into the project that our project
was staffed at a level that might support only four or five campuses. The fact
that we had active engagement at nine campuses represented a step forward,
an opportunity to learn more together about how to use action inquiry to
address critical challenges.

In addition to providing workshops on a method of inquiry, the IPAS
team provided technical assistance with the inquiry process. This assistance

Table 5.1. Challenges Chosen for Action Inquiry at Partner Campuses

Partner Campus	Campus Type	Critical Challenges
Indiana University Northwest	Four-year regional, public	1. Undecided students 2. Supplemental instruction 3. Critical Literacy Program (remedial students) 4. Working students
Purdue University Calumet	Four-year regional, public	1. Working students 2. Supplemental instruction 3. Academic Recovery Program
Ivy Tech Northwest	Two-year, public	1. First-Year Experience 2. Working students 3. Tutoring
Indiana Wesleyan	Four-year, private	1. Center for Life Calling and Leadership
Indiana University East	Four-year regional, public	1. 21st Century Scholars 2. Sophomore persistence
Ivy Tech Richmond	Two-year, public	1. Remedial education 2. Financial aid 3. Academic support
IUPUI	Four-year regional, public	1. Transfer program 2. Diversity and curriculum
Indiana University Kokomo	Four-year regional, public	1. Learning communities
Ivy Tech Central	Two-year, public	1. Diverse students 2. Academic advising 3. IR capacity building 4. Transfer program

included involvement at meetings on the campuses, writing literature reviews for campus teams exploring topics or to summarize research on best practices, holding and analyzing focus group interviews, and conducting evaluation analyses that used data merged from campus records and the state data system. This ongoing technical assistance was invaluable to the process and made it possible for the willing to make progress.

Case Examples

During the 2004–05 academic year, workgroups on the nine campuses engaged in inquiry on the challenge topics. The extent of involvement varied. One relatively small, multicampus community college—Ivy Tech Northwest—was intensively involved, as were workgroups at other campuses. Many of the issues addressed by the working groups dealt with responding to the needs of students differently than in the past and started with building an understanding of the problem.

Two forms of building an understanding of a challenge emerged among the campuses, as shown in Figure 5.2. When workgroups chose challenge areas with a history, it was often possible to start with the evaluation process, creating a mini-inquiry. However, when the problems were new, then the workgroups started at the beginning of the cycle and looped through the inquiry process. Although most campuses chose local challenges, a few instances of multicampus collaboration emerged. Three patterns emerged among the working groups:

- Inquiry into challenge areas with a history at the campus, a process that started with an evaluation of current practice (see the small loop in Figure 5.2)
- Inquiry into new topics for which there was little or no history of intervention, necessitating that inquiry be started from the beginning (see the big loop in Figure 5.2)
- Collaboration in addressing challenges shared across campuses, starting either with evaluation of current practice or with building an understanding of new challenges.

Examples of the Evaluation Loop

Indiana University Kokomo (IUK) had implemented a set of connected courses for first-year students as part of an earlier retention project that had received funding from the IU system. They had modified the learning community concept for commuter students, the clients of this regional campus that did not have dormitories. From the initial workshop on IPAS, the IUK team focused on the evaluation of this venture. The IPAS team conducted focus group interviews with students and a multivariate study of the intervention on retention (described in Chapter Six of this volume). These

Figure 5.2. Role of Preliminary Evaluation in the IPAS Process for the Short Loop Through Inquiry

mixed-method evaluation results were important for the campus because the special funding would soon expire and the results could help them with decisions about whether and how to continue with this program, given their budget constraints.

Indiana Wesleyan University chose to focus on a program they had developed to support students who were undecided about their majors. The multiyear process involved exploring personal purpose and interests during the first college year, different forms of engaged learning and leadership during the sophomore and junior years, and job options during the senior year. This project had been funded by the Lilly Endowment and was nearing completion, so it was time to evaluate. In addition, they had had inquiries about their model from many other campuses. They concentrated their IPAS activities on this distinctive program, using IPAS staff to conduct focus group interviews and to complete the multivariate study of the type described in Chapter Six of this volume. The results are being used by the campus in communication with other campuses about their model as well as in internal decisions about the future of the program.

These examples illustrate the small-loop process. By starting with evaluation, the collaborative effort helped to close the loop on prior innovations, building an understanding of possible next steps. In fact, as discussed in Chapter Six, multivariate studies of persistence were conducted for each of the IU campuses as part of the IPAS funding agreement. These evaluations provided information for summer workshops for participants at partner campuses.

Too frequently, campuses that engage in innovations during a grant period have difficulty reallocating internal resources to continue the effort after external funding ends. Integrating sound evaluation methods into the process can inform decision making about whether to continue, how to modify, and how to fund these projects if they have their intended effects.

Using the Full Inquiry Cycle

Many of the workgroups addressed new challenges. In these instances, campus teams formed to address challenge areas, starting with the process of building a shared understanding of the problem.

IVY Tech Richmond, a small, two-year college in Richmond, Indiana, focused on challenges related to access and outreach for diverse students, use of state and federal student aid funds, and student understanding of their choices in a college environment. After exploring these challenges, they realized that academic literacy was central to each of these issues. After considering a range of options and realizing that funding was limited, they decided to try out—or pilot test—a new orientation process. Historically, the campus had done very little to inform new students. They designed an orientation that included information on student aid, registration, support services, and related topics. They planned a new orientation for admitted students and designed an instrument to measure student knowledge of the topics covered. They administered the instrument as a pretest and posttest for the new orientation, building baseline for judging how well they did with the new program.

Indiana University-Purdue University Indianapolis (IUPUI) formed a workgroup composed of faculty members from different academic fields who were interested in persistence by diverse students, a topic that had emerged from the review of IPAS research. During 2004–05 the group met with a facilitator to discuss alternative approaches to current practices. By the end of the year, the workgroup had designed interventions for their courses during the next years. Some had designed their own research projects and secured human subject approval for classroom research during the 2005–06 academic years. In addition, the IPAS team worked with the facilitator to provide research support—interviews and quantitative analyses—that could provide evaluations of the process.

As these examples illustrate, not all of the projects would be implemented on a scale that would allow for multivariate statistical analyses and evaluation. Nevertheless, workgroups were encouraged to integrate evaluation into the design of their interventions to understand the effectiveness of their interventions and to plan modifications for future improvements.

Multicampus Collaborations

During several IPAS workshops involving the three campuses in northwestern Indiana and the regional IU campus in South Bend, administrators at the three Gary-region campuses—Purdue University Calumet, IU Northwest, and Ivy Tech Northwest—formed a collaborative workgroup to address a common challenge: providing educational opportunities for working students. Unlike students at the major state college and research university campuses in the state, students at these campuses tended to be workers first and students second. The team from Purdue Calumet was the first to focus on the issue and chose to evaluate their efforts to employ students in supplemental instruction activities, one of their topical areas. As workshop conversations progressed, a collaborative team emerged with members from the three Gary-region campuses. For many years, there had been interest in collaborative projects in the region but none had emerged before IPAS.

The workgroup planned a conference to discuss the challenge, with participation from the three campuses. Then they secured funding from their campuses to conduct a survey of working students to learn about their working situations, their course preferences, and whether they had support for college enrollment. In addition to cosponsoring the conference, the IPAS team completed a literature review on working students (Tuttle, McKinney, and Rago, 2005), a resource that proved helpful in the survey design. This collaboration illustrates sustained effort to build an understanding of a shared problem. Over the longer term, the workgroup hoped to secure support from local businesses and other groups for new programs. However, they realized that their first step involved finding out more about this unique group of students for which there was only limited information from prior students.

The other example of collaboration involved IUPUI and Ivy Tech Indianapolis. While IUPUI had a well-established IR function, they did not have access to data on transfer students. They decided to form an IPAS workgroup with Ivy Tech to evaluate their new collaborative admissions arrangements. Historically, IUPUI had functioned as a nearly open-admissions institution, with a high drop-out rate attributable to academic failures. After the Ivy Tech system began to transition to community college status, IUPUI raised admissions standards. IUPUI referred some applicants to Ivy Tech and delayed admissions until after completion of a preparatory program.

The new workgroup started with a review of this new admissions arrangement. To support this collaborative workgroup, the IPAS team analyzed the college enrollment patterns of students who had been deferred from IUPUI for academic reasons, building a basic descriptive understanding of the impact of the new admissions procedure. In addition, IPAS convened a statewide meeting on articulation and transfer with an external consultant to facilitate a shared understanding of best practice. With this background, the workgroup began the process of exploring the next steps that could be taken to build on this foundation.

From Inquiry to Action

At the midpoint of an action research project, it simply is not possible to reach summative conclusions. In particular, we do not yet know if the project will encourage or enable change at the participating campuses or if the model can be replicated—though we would like to think we will achieve these aims. A great deal has been learned, even if we are uncertain about the ultimate outcomes. At this point, we can only summarize what we have learned about research-informed reform.

NEW DIRECTIONS FOR INSTITUTIONAL RESEARCH • DOI: 10.1002/ir

It is evident that an inquiry model has been used by some campuses to address the challenges they identified. Three major themes seem to run through the efforts, all of which relate to the extensive research conducted with the state database. One theme is supporting diversity on the campuses. There is a growing realization that there is a need to focus on the core academic mission, from the academic literacy of first-generation students (the Ivy Tech Richmond project) to engagement of faculty in innovations in their courses (IUPUI faculty workgroup). Second, many of the new students coming to Indiana campuses are from working-class families. Efforts to engage students on campuses (IU Kokomo learning communities) and to study working students on their own terms (the northwestern region collaboration) illustrate new ventures aimed at addressing the learning needs of this new clientele. Finally, the integration of formal evaluation as a capstone activity for innovative projects represented a major step forward for most of the campuses in the state.

The current challenge for IPAS is to design interventions that can be pilot tested and evaluated by the end of the project. An intensive effort is now being made (summer 2005) to refine plans for interventions. To complete the process as originally envisioned, more of the collaborating campuses will need to move through the action planning process, to implement new innovative projects as pilot tests that can be evaluated. The intent of the project has been to implement well-designed interventions during the 2005–06 academic year, enabling data collection as an integral part of the evaluations (interviews along with empirical data on participation), so that it will be possible to complete a new set of evaluations of students during the final term of the three-year project (fall term of 2006). Whether or not new projects will be implemented during this time frame still remains to be seen.

One of the major lessons learned from the project is that inquiry involves collaboration between institutional researchers and campus workgroups. The pattern of learning at the campuses has been enhanced by collaborations with researchers from the IPAS team. During the summer of 2005 a statewide workshop was conducted that provided opportunities for the collaborating campuses to present the results of their work to date. Some had completed a complete inquiry cycle, while others were still trying to get started. However, it was clear by the end of the meeting that most of the successful ventures had involved collaborations between campus groups and IPAS researchers who provided technical assistance. The collaborative nature of the project reflected the spirit of collaboration advocated by Hansen and Borden in Chapter Four of this volume. Indeed, after a year and a half we had come full circle. (The papers presented as Chapters One, Two, and Four of this volume had been presented at the initial workshop in January 2004. The issues—limited use of formal evaluation and the need for collaboration—had been discussed extensively, often in heated ways.) At the outset we had understood, conceptually at least, that the project was collaboration. By the midpoint, the summer of 2005, the meaning of and potential for collaboration were understood in a more practical way by one and all. It was

NEW DIRECTIONS FOR INSTITUTIONAL RESEARCH • DOI: 10.1002/ir

no longer theory. Most of us understood that the breakthrough resulted from the collaboration. The new ideas came from efforts to understand past efforts coupled with critical thinking about the real lives of students.

A second lesson relates to evaluation, another starting point for the project understood better with time. At the initial meeting in January 2004, there was a division between researchers and practitioners. The data were somewhat intimidating to practitioners who lacked training in statistics. And the graduate students and researchers were not yet engaged. By the summer of 2005, when a new set of evaluations was presented, most of the participants understood the importance of the work. Many practitioners spoke about how the literature reviews and evaluation results were being used in decision-making processes on campuses. The researchers had come to understand the utility of applied research. It was no longer ethereal; both practitioners and researchers shared a commitment to working together, at least so it seemed as the midproject meeting came to a close.

Finally, it is also evident that the state-level databases have substantial value for research on college students, but there is a need to use research to support change and improvement. The Indiana Commission for Higher Education had for many years collected student records with information on high school curriculum, SAT scores, and college majors, grades, and student aid. There had been a few prior studies using these data, but their potential utility had not been fully tapped. As part of IPAS, this database was used for state- and campus-level analyses. Campuses could compare their results to those of the state as a whole. They could also explore new topics, such as transfer and retention by minority students. While the many tables generated in the process usually did not captivate the interest of practitioners, the new bottom lines—the findings—generally were understood. It was relatively easy to pick up a few key points from both sets of analyses. Typically, these understandings were situated within the interests of the individuals and sometimes were commonly understood among team members. But more important, it became evident that research could help practitioners build an understanding of the challenges about which they had nagging concerns, providing the starting point for inquiry.

References

Allen, W. R., Epps, E. G., and Haniff, N. Z. (eds.). *College in Black and White: African American Students in Predominantly White and in Historically Black Public Universities.* Albany, N.Y.: SUNY Press, 1991.

Balderston, F. E. *Managing Today's University.* San Francisco: Jossey-Bass, 1974.

Banta, T. W., Rudolph, C. B., Van Dyke, J., and Fisher, H. S. "Performance Funding Comes of Age in Tennessee." *Journal of Higher Education,* 1996, 67, 23–45.

Chaffee, E. E. "Role of Rationality in University Budgeting." *Research in Higher Education,* 1983, 19(4), 387–406.

Cheit, E. F. *The New Depression in Higher Education: Two Years Later.* New York: McGraw Hill, 1974.

Habermas, J. *Theory of Communicative Action.* Vol. 1: *Reason and the Rationalization of Society.* Boston: Beacon Press, 1984.

Habermas, J. *The Theory of Communicative Action.* Vol. 2: *Lifeworld and System: A Critique of Functionalist Reasoning* (T. McCarthy, trans.). Boston: Beacon Press, 1987.

Habermas, J. *The Structural Transformation of the Public Sphere: An Inquiry into a Category of Bourgeois Society.* Cambridge, Mass.: MIT Press, 1991.

Halstead, D. K. *Statewide Planning in Higher Education.* Washington, D.C.: U.S. Government Printing Office, 1974.

Keller, G. *Academic Strategy: The Management Revolution in American Higher Education.* Baltimore: Johns Hopkins University Press, 1983.

Norris, P. M., and Poulton, N. L. *A Guide for New Planners.* Ann Arbor: Society for College and University Planning, 1987.

Paulsen, M. B., and St. John, E. P. "Budget Incentive Structures and the Improvement of College Teaching." In D. M. Priest and others (eds.), *Incentive-Based Budgeting Systems in Public Universities.* Northampton, Mass.: Edward Elgar, 2002.

St. John, E. P. *Prices, Productivity, and Investment: Assessing Financial Strategies in Higher Education.* ASHE-ERIC Higher Education Report, no. 3. Washington, D.C.: George Washington University, School of Education and Human Development, 1994.

St. John, E. P. "Rethinking Tuition and Student Aid Strategies." In E. P. St. John (ed.), *Rethinking Tuition and Student Aid Strategies.* New Directions for Higher Education, no. 89. San Francisco: Jossey-Bass, 1995.

St. John, E. P. *Refinancing the College Dream: Access, Equal Opportunity, and Justice for Taxpayers.* Baltimore: Johns Hopkins University Press, 2003.

St. John, E. P., Carter, D. F., Chung, C. G., and Musoba, G. D. "Diversity and Persistence in Indiana Higher Education: The Impact of Preparation, Major Choices, and Student Aid." In E. P. St. John (ed.), *Readings on Equal Education.* Vol. 21: *Public Policy and Educational Opportunity: School Reforms, Postsecondary Encouragement, and State Policies on Higher Education* (pp. 359–410). New York: AMS Press, 2006.

Thomas, G. E. "College Major and Career Inequality: Implications for Black Students." *Journal of Negro Education,* 1985, *54,* 537–547.

Tuttle, T., McKinney, J., and Rago, M. *College Students Working: The Choice Nexus—A Review of Research Literature on College Students and Work.* IPAS Topic Brief. Bloomington: Indiana Project on Academic Success, 2005.

Weathersby, G. B., and Balderston, F. E. "PPBS in Higher Education Planning and Management: Part I, An Overview." *Higher Education,* 1972, *1,* 191–206.

EDWARD P. ST. JOHN *is Algo D. Henderson Collegiate Professor of Education at the Center for the Study of Higher and Postsecondary Education at the University of Michigan. His research focuses on educational policy and public finance in both K-12 and higher education.*

JEFFREY S. MCKINNEY *is associate director of the Indiana Project on Academic Success. He holds a Ph.D. in higher education and student affairs from Indiana University.*

TINA TUTTLE, *a former student services administrator, is a doctoral candidate at Indiana University with research interests in college access, working students, nontraditional adult students, student financial aid, and veterans' educational attainment.*

NEW DIRECTIONS FOR INSTITUTIONAL RESEARCH • DOI: 10.1002/ir

6

Evaluation can provide the assessment information for considering program change as well as be integral to the program design and pilot test of any new institutional intervention.

Using Evaluation to Close the Inquiry Loop

Glenda Droogsma Musoba

Evaluation is generally thought of as the responsibility of the institutional research (IR) office and is too often considered an afterthought rather than an integral part of program administration. The relationship between the IR office and campus academic and student affairs practitioners is often limited to traditional evaluation practices, typically when the IR office is called in to conduct an evaluation of an existing program. To complicate this relationship, the evaluation can be accompanied by some resistance or fear among practitioners that their job performance is also being evaluated. Although administrators have endorsed the value of assessment, too often, pressing work responsibilities, limited expertise, and inaccessible or inadequate data mean evaluation is a "should have" or an afterthought, and administrators making important program decisions have to rely on professional intuition or on evaluations that are of limited quality and usefulness.

Simultaneously, IR offices often do not have the luxury of data, time, and staff to conduct the rigorous evaluations they envision. For example, retention evaluations are often limited to disaggregated comparisons without controlling for other factors known to be associated with persistence. The examination by Braxton, McKinney, and Reynolds in Chapter Two of this volume suggests that only a few IR studies in Indiana have met the standard of rigor to be considered publishable research. IR staff members often believe they are caught in a dilemma between conducting rigorous studies of limited usefulness or conducting studies that provide practical information for administrators but do not meet research standards of rigor. These

NEW DIRECTIONS FOR INSTITUTIONAL RESEARCH, no. 130, Summer 2006 © Wiley Periodicals, Inc.
Published online in Wiley InterScience (www.interscience.wiley.com) • DOI: 10.1002/ir.181

problems are not new to the IR professional. However, there are functional approaches to evaluation developed through persistence research that can provide rigorous evidence for campus program evaluation. While not resolving all the issues, evaluation within an inquiry process offers some potential solutions to this situation.

Evaluation in an action inquiry cycle can use the workable models approach initially developed and advanced by St. John (1992) to test the relationship between financial aid and student persistence. Theoretically grounded in sociologic, economic, and higher education theory and research, the workable models approach has been successfully used in a number of institutional and state-level studies of persistence (Hu and St. John, 2001; St. John, 1999; St. John, Hu, and Weber, 2000, 2001; St. John, Simmons, and Musoba, 2002; Somers and St. John, 1997; Somers, Woodhouse, and Cofer, 2004). The workable models approach advocates using existing institutional individual student records that provide student demographics, academic preparation, and other data, combined with program participation to test the influence on persistence or other student outcomes of the program while controlling for other individual student differences. This approach is both rigorous and practical. Moreover, data are often already collected through admissions and enrollment records, making the approach practical.

In Chapter Four of this volume, Hansen and Borden illustrate the action inquiry approach using qualitative methods; the workable models approach is a more quantitative process. Both qualitative and quantitative methods fit well with the inquiry process and are essential. Depending on the research needs of the institution staff, the two approaches offer different information and are useful at different points.

Within an inquiry framework, IR professionals and practitioners collaborate in an inquiry process that integrates evaluation into program planning and design. Evaluation's primary function is to finish the inquiry cycle; when challenges are not met, evaluation findings become the assessment data in a subsequent loop of the inquiry cycle. As Figure 5.1 in Chapter Five of this volume shows, evaluation is the last step in the inquiry cycle. Yet it is not only a last step; as the example in this chapter will illustrate, evaluation evidence is used throughout the inquiry process. Evaluation provides evidence for institutional decision making rather than a cumulative assessment of success or failure. As will be illustrated, evaluation evidence can be used during assessment while building an understanding of the challenge as part of planning and implementing a pilot test.

Any evaluation outcome is a learning success for the campus workgroup. If the evaluation documents that the campus program positively addresses the identified challenge—and therefore some measure of student performance, such as persistence, is improved—program administrators know the program is useful and have the evidence to justify ongoing program funding to senior administrators, and institutions have useful information for ongoing planning. In some instances, institutions can make further incremental improvements to the program based on their evaluation findings.

Alternatively, if the program shows no relationship with student success associated with the identified challenge, then administrators have learned from the pilot test that they will need an alternative strategy. The institution will not be wasting money on an ineffective program, and resources can be reallocated to serve students better. In this mindset, a negative outcome for the program is not seen as a failure, with jobs at stake, but as successful learning, because the campus staff will have learned more about the challenge, and the lack of success may suggest an alternative strategy. The administrators will know they need to cycle through the inquiry process again because the challenge has not been met. The evaluation becomes the assessment evidence for the next loop through the cycle.

Finally, if the campus program shows no improvement on indicators related to the identified challenge but does have unintended positive outcomes, administrators may choose to continue the program, but they will have the evidence that the initial campus challenge remains. For example, a program may improve retention for first-generation students even though the intervention was designed to help low-income students. The program may be maintained, but it will not be maintained on false premises. The decision makers or campus workgroup will want to cycle through the action inquiry process again to address the identified challenge. Again, the learning from the pilot test and evaluation is valued and the results of the evaluation become the assessment for the next time through the inquiry cycle.

Evaluation in the IPAS Inquiry-Based Process

The inquiry approach we have advocated in the Indiana Project on Academic Success (IPAS) has been an evidence-rich process throughout all the steps. Our dual goals have included improving student success by addressing a critical challenge and creating a more evidence-based decision-making culture on the campuses. We wanted to test whether this inquiry approach would bring about institutional change for students and help practitioners become more sophisticated consumers of research. If we were successful, campus IR offices would become more integral to decision making and campus practitioners would be asking IR offices for more evaluative evidence of the effectiveness of their programs or even asking for evidence before designing a program. Based on the meta-analysis by Braxton, McKinney, and Reynolds described in Chapter Two of this volume, we knew rigorous program evaluation was not happening regularly on our partner campuses.

As campuses develop pilot tests of program interventions, evaluation is necessary to determine the effectiveness of the programs and interventions. Although evaluation evidence can be used throughout the inquiry process, its primary role is to close the inquiry loop. Inquiry falls apart without the evaluation step. If a pilot test does not include inquiry, it is just "starting small" and is not a real pilot test. Evaluation is philosophically and practically essential in an evidence-based approach to campus change.

In the IPAS Campus Inquiry Model, evaluation is considered not only at the end of the inquiry cycle but is integrated into each of the steps of the inquiry loop. Table 6.1 illustrates the relationship between evaluation and the other stages.

In the assessment stage of inquiry, while campus administrators identify a critical challenge to student success, the student outcomes variable, or as we termed it "the critical success indicator," which will be the standard against which the program will be evaluated, is also identified. This

Table 6.1. The Role of Evaluation in IPAS

Stage	Strategies	Outcome(s)
Stage 1 Assess	• Identify possible challenges • Collect and analyze data • Prioritize challenges • Organize work groups	• Identify critical success indicators for challenges (outcome measures)
Stage 2 Organize	• Coordinate budgeting to provide necessary support • Appoint IPAS Scholars • Coordinate inquiry with campus planning and budgeting	• Identify targets of opportunity for improvement

Stage 3
Conduct Action
Inquiry
	• Each campus workgroup engages in a process with the following goals:
	  1. Build an understanding of the challenge
	  2. Look internally and externally for solutions
	  3. Assess possible solutions
	  4. Develop action plans
	  5. Implement pilot test and evaluate
		• Design interventions and evaluations
		• Use evaluation methods that provide information about critical success indicators

Stage 4 Evaluation	• Campus teams coordinate implementation and evaluation: provide reviews of plans; encourage presentations to campus planning groups; facilitate coordination of inquiry process with campus planning • Coordinate evaluation support of pilot tests with IPAS teams and campus groups	• Consider implications for planning, budgeting, and practice in future years

establishes and makes clear which student population and what student outcome are being addressed. Quantitatively, this is often defined as a significant numeric improvement in student persistence, but it could also be improved student GPA, which is related to student persistence. Qualitatively, the campus might be evaluating how a particular program was aiding student success. Defining the goal early in the process helps campus teams keep focused on the challenge rather than on other possibly worthy goals.

Because of time constraints in our own process, although we did not introduce evaluation in the initial meeting, we introduced evaluation just a few months into the process. On one campus, the campus team's discussion of the specific student outcome they wanted to improve was instrumental to their building a basic understanding of their challenge. This focus was maintained as they were evaluating possible solutions in the inquiry stage. Specifically, although they knew their students were not taking advantage of campus academic support resources that the students needed, it was the workgroup's definition of success as "students being more sophisticated in the academic experience" that clarified their goals for their intervention, including having as part of their definition student knowledge wherever they attended rather than just persistence at their institution. The definition of the critical success indicator makes for an objective and measurable outcome with a defined timeline. For example, a campus could define its success indicator as a 3 percent increase in retention from the first to the second year for undecided students (those who have not chosen a major) or a significant difference in persistence between undecided students who participated in a program and those who did not.

In the organization stage, evaluation helps focus on individuals or departments that must be represented in the process. In the example of retention of undecided students, this definition of success suggests that both academic advising staff and someone with research expertise might be necessary members of a workgroup.

In the inquiry stage, evaluation is intimately linked to pilot test design. Philosophically, it is important to maintain an experimental approach in the later stages of inquiry when designing an intervention. If the intervention is designed without a sense of evaluation and inquiry, it is in danger of being solidified into a campus program whether useful or not. Too often, as developers of programs, administrators become invested in their ideas and certain of their value. Although not tested, I speculate that this natural inclination may be even stronger when we have taken such an intentional inquiry-based approach to program development. Therefore, designing interventions coupled with evaluation is important. The evaluation design may dominate the pilot test when administrative cultures require more experimental methodologies. In other campus cultures, it may only be necessary to define how participation data will be collected, and the evaluation may have only limited influence on the pilot test design. The audience of the evaluation may be most important in defining this balance.

NEW DIRECTIONS FOR INSTITUTIONAL RESEARCH • DOI: 10.1002/ir

During the actual evaluation stage, campus teams will need to collect and analyze the data, prepare a report of the findings, and disseminate those findings to the relevant audiences. In some instances this evaluation may be formative for the campus workgroup and will be used to finish the inquiry cycle. In other instances, administrators or outside funding agencies are the intended audience of the evaluation. Ideally, in an environment where learning is valued—a lack of program success is defined as learning in this situation—the report would not be any different between the workgroup and external audiences. Part of the IPAS goal has been to encourage this learning culture on our partner campuses.

Evaluation in an inquiry-based process, as shown in Figure 5.1 in the previous chapter, requires engagement of a campus team beyond the IR office. This collective learning requires an active engagement between the researcher and practitioner. Traditional program evaluation can be an important part of the learning in this process but is distinct from evaluation as part of a learning loop. Figure 5.2 in Chapter Five illustrates a more traditional approach to program evaluation and was used in a number of instances with our partner campuses. This more traditional approach to evaluation can be done independently by the IR office. On several campuses, when challenges were identified, there were existing programs on the campuses intended to address the challenges, but no evaluation had been conducted on those programs. Therefore, the short loop from identification of a challenge to program evaluation was conducted before the campus workgroups could cycle through the full inquiry-based approach. This evaluation immediately became assessment data to help the campus team build an understanding of the challenge.

While a couple of the campuses had established IR offices doing inferential statistical analyses, evaluation as part of inquiry following the workable models approach was new to most of our campuses. Therefore, we knew evaluation needed to be integral to the process, and we introduced it early to our workgroups. To meet our goal of encouraging a more inquiry-based decision-making process, it was important to help administrators and practitioners become more sophisticated consumers and potential producers of data. If they did not already know it, they needed to see the value of inferential statistics and other research approaches that considered the complexity of student experiences in program evaluation. In the assessment stage, we introduced the IPAS inquiry-based process along with statewide and campus-specific assessment data on student persistence to help the campuses identify challenges to student success. These regression analyses, using the workable models approach, provided campus-specific evidence of challenges as well as examples of the type of research evidence that was obtainable with their campus data for the evaluation of possible future pilot tests.

Although evaluation was officially the final step, data—both quantitative and qualitative—were infused throughout the cycle. As mentioned earlier, in the assessment stage, we provided campus-specific analyses of persistence. While each campus was building an understanding of their challenges during the inquiry stage, we encouraged campus workgroups to collect evidence about their students and campus, either from existing or new data. This was intended to sustain an inquiry-based approach, yet evidence in the form of program evaluation is particularly important in relation to any pilot-tested interventions.

Case Study from the Indiana Project on Academic Success

A case study example illustrates how evaluation was used on IPAS partner campuses. This particular example, which I will call "Region University" (RU), provides an example of how evaluation was used in the short loop, but the same evaluation approach will be used with their future interventions. RU's campus workgroup realized the university had a campus program designed to address the campus challenge—increasing persistence by first-generation students—but they had never evaluated whether the program was positively addressing the challenge.

RU is a regional campus of one of the two state flagship universities in Indiana. RU serves a mixed student population that is more likely to be first-generation, part-time, nontraditional age, and less prepared academically than typical students enrolled at the main flagship campuses. RU offers a variety of major programs of study at a commuter campus that enrolls fewer than ten thousand students. In 2002, with faculty and administrators concerned about students' academic engagement and persistence, RU introduced first-year student learning communities as a retention initiative. At this campus, year-long learning communities are defined as two linked courses each semester of the first year. Participation is optional for students, but learning community courses fill core curriculum requirements. For example, in the fall semester, English composition and a humanities core course are cotaught by faculty from both departments, with shared assignments and content under a shared topic. In the spring semester, speech and a social-behavioral science are linked. After initial implementation, linked courses were also developed in math and science, and an example of a recent learning-community topic is "love." Classes were designed to promote connections among students, between students and faculty, and to aid the transition to college. Participating faculty members were enthusiastic about the experience and the students. Informal feedback was positive, but a rigorous evaluation of the relationship between participation in learning communities and student success had not been conducted.

When RU joined the IPAS project, they had continuing concerns about students' transitions to college and persistence, particularly for students who had dependents or who had not declared a major. It became a natural early step for their campus workgroup to ask whether the learning communities were effective. They chose a two-fold approach to evaluation. First, the IPAS team conducted the quantitative evaluation described in this

New Directions for Institutional Research • DOI: 10.1002/ir

section. In addition, on behalf of RU, IPAS staff conducted focus group interviews with students currently in learning communities and one year out of learning communities as well as interviews of faculty who taught in the learning communities. This combination of quantitative and qualitative data provided a full evaluation and was the primary source of information for the RU workgroup in assessing progress and building an understanding of their challenge. A brief summary of the quantitative evaluation follows, beginning with an explanation of the evaluation methodology used for this campus and for most of the IPAS campuses.

Methodology. Data for this analysis were from several sources. Existing institutional individual-level data, provided through the Indiana Commission for Higher Education, were matched with individual-level records on student participation or frequency of participation in the pilot test program provided by the campus workgroup. Student retention—defined as persistence from the fall to the spring semester for first-year students—was the outcome variable; therefore, a logistic regression with this dichotomous outcome was appropriate. This analysis used the workable models approach to control for student characteristics known through prior research to be associated with the outcome. Because extant data often have missing values that in many instances like this one are not randomly distributed, the workable models approach uses categorical coding of variables with missing data as a category, thus retaining all cases in the regression model and allowing for interpretation of the results to the full sample—in this instance, first-year students at the campus. Despite the limitation in the difficulty of interpreting the meaning of the missing data category, the approach is better than the systematic bias and lost cases of the alternative.

Individual-level variables and their coding are shown in Table 6.2. Variables are included for student demographic characteristics, academic preparation, college experience, financial aid, and—the variable of most interest in these models—participation in the pilot test program. Regression simultaneously considers these characteristics that prior research has shown to be associated with persistence along with the participation variable, therefore separating out the unique influence of each on persistence.

Student participation in several other campus programs thought also to be associated with persistence was included in the model as well. For RU, we included enrollment intensity (full- or part-time), college GPA, college major, financial aid package, and participation in developmental coursework. (In this analysis, financial aid package represents both the financial aid the student received and a measure of family income or need. The four aid/income status categories included those students with the highest financial need, Pell grant recipients, students eligible for grants but not eligible for Pell, students who did not receive grants but did receive some other form of financial aid such as loans, and students who did not receive any aid either because of ineligibility due to income or a failure to apply for aid.) In addition, for RU we included variables for frequency of participation in supplemental

Table 6.2. Variable Coding and Descriptive Statistics for Variables in Region University's Regression Model for Persistence of Fall to Spring Semester by First-Year Students in Year 2002

Variable	Category	N	Col %
	Persisters	493	61.70
	Nonpersisters	306	38.30
Age	Age under 21©	488	61.08
	Age 21–24	116	14.52
	Age 25–29	77	9.64
	Age 30 and over	118	14.77
Gender	Male	433	54.19
	Female©	366	45.81
Ethnicity	Native American	3	0.38
	Asian American Pacific Islander	9	1.13
	African American	27	3.38
	Hispanic	17	2.13
	White©	719	89.99
	Missing	24	3.00
Dependency Status	Indeterminate status	357	44.68
	Self-supporting©	156	19.52
	Dependent	286	35.79
High School GPA	A	5	0.63
	B	26	3.25
	C or Less©	85	10.64
	Missing	683	85.48
High School Diploma	Honors	12	1.50
	Core 40	71	8.89
	Regular or Missing©	716	89.61
Major in Fall 2002	Humanities	22	2.75
	Science and Math	26	3.25
	Social Science	48	6.01
	Health	166	20.78
	Business	90	11.26
	Education	73	9.14
	Computer	8	1.00
	Engineering	1	0.13
	Others	104	13.02
	Undecided©	261	32.67
College GPA	A	138	17.27
	B©	319	39.92
	C or Less	321	40.18
	Missing	21	2.63
Remedial Coursework	Remedial Math only	242	30.29
	Remedial Language Arts only	29	3.63
	Remedial Math and Language Arts	38	4.76
	No Remedial Coursework©	490	61.33
Full-time enrollment in Fall 2002	Part-time	383	47.93
	Full-time	416	52.07

(continued)

NEW DIRECTIONS FOR INSTITUTIONAL RESEARCH • DOI: 10.1002/ir

Table 6.2. (continued)

Variable	Category	N	Col %
Frequency of participation in Supplemental Instruction	Not in an SI Course©	634	79.35
	Never had SI but in an SI course	111	13.89
	SI one to three times	31	3.88
	SI four or more times	23	2.88
Frequency of participation in tutoring	Did not receive tutoring©	714	89.36
	One to three times	53	6.63
	More than three times	32	4.01
Participated in a course offering supplemental instruction	Not in an SI Course©	634	79.35
	Yes, in an SI course	165	20.65
Participation in a learning community	Not in a learning community©	685	85.73
	In a learning community	114	14.27
Aid/income status	No financial aid©	347	43.43
	Other aid recipient, including loans	227	28.41
	Other need-based grant recipient	11	1.38
	Pell recipient	214	26.78
Total		799	100.00

©This symbol represents the comparison group in the regression analysis. Variables in the model are interpreted in relation to this group.

instruction and frequency with which the student took advantage of campus-provided academic tutoring services. Although these programs were not the primary impetus for the evaluation for the campus workgroup, the team believed they were also important for student persistence and academic success related to student retention. The inclusion of these data controlled for the simultaneous participation in these programs by some students. This step was necessary so that discrete comparisons were made in the analysis. Regression findings (odds ratios) are presented in two models. The first model does not include the program participation variables; the second model does. The two models allow for examination of interactions between student characteristics and participation in the programs.

Limitations. There are several limitations to this approach. As discussed earlier, when working with existing data the researcher does not control the data quality and missing values. For individual campuses using this approach with their campus data, this limitation may be less substantial. In addition, when dealing with existing data, there are often other variables that the researcher would like to include in the model but that are unavailable. Students often participate simultaneously in multiple campus programs and other events outside the campus experience that influence their persistence. These factors in persistence are left out of the existing model. This limitation is true in virtually all persistence research, making it not unique to this study. However, the inferential statistical approach represented here is far superior to simple comparisons of persistence rates or a *t*-test comparing participants and nonparticipants without controlling for other student characteristics. (Although we advocate for the inferential statistical approach when appropriate, it should be noted that for some of our partner campuses the pilot-tested intervention does not lend itself to regression analysis—for example, extremely small samples—and we are also using focus groups or other qualitative approaches.)

Finally, this analysis is limited to within-year persistence of the first year, although longer-term persistence is also of interest. As additional data become available, persistence into later years or to graduation should also be considered.

Findings. Descriptive statistics for the first-year students in Tables 6.2 and 6.3 show comparisons in persistence for variables in the regression analysis. Overall, the within-year persistence rate at RU was 62 percent for first-year students. Approximately 14 percent of students classified as first-year students participated in one of the voluntary learning communities. About 20 percent of the students were in a course offering supplemental instruction, but only about 7 percent of all students took advantage of the service. Just over 6 percent of first-year students attended tutoring a few times, while 4 percent attended four or more times. About one-third of the first-year students had not declared a major, and almost 40 percent of the first-year students were over twenty-one years of age. Just fewer than 40 percent took at least one course in developmental math or language arts. Slightly more than half of the students attended full time.

The results of the persistence regression analysis are presented in Table 6.4. Findings regarding the campus programs will be discussed first, followed by other findings regarding first-year students at RU.

Students who participated in a learning community in their fall semester were more than twice as likely (2.687 odds ratio) to persist from the fall to the spring semester, controlling for all other variables in the model. This was a particularly strong finding in the model. Clearly, at this commuter campus, learning communities are having a positive impact on students' retention.

There was no significant difference between students who took advantage of supplemental instruction (SI) and students who were not enrolled in courses offering supplemental instruction. A subsequent analysis not included here of the relationship between SI and students' course grades showed that students who took advantage of SI up to three times had higher grades than students who did not seek out SI. Students who used SI more than three times did not have significantly different grades than students who did not use the additional support. The fact that students who found the class challenging enough to seek help were not getting lower grades suggests that a nonsignificant finding here may have practical significance for students.

Students who sought out the help of the tutoring center but only did so a few times persisted at a higher rate than students who never sought tutoring. These may have been successful students who wanted additional support to enhance their grades, or they may have been students who

Table 6.3. Persistence Rates of Fall to Spring Semester by First-Year Students in 2002 for Variables in the Regression Analysis for Region University

Variable	Category	Persisters		Nonpersisters	
		N	Row %	N	Row %
Age	Age under 21	336	68.9	152	31.1
	Age 21–24	47	40.5	69	59.5
	Age 25–29	42	54.5	35	45.5
	Age 30 and over	68	57.6	50	42.4
Gender	Male	281	64.9	152	35.1
	Female	212	57.9	154	42.1
Ethnicity	Native American	2	66.7	1	33.3
	Asian American Pacific Islander	5	55.6	4	44.4
	African American	13	48.1	14	51.9
	Hispanic	7	41.2	10	58.8
	White	452	62.9	267	37.1
	Missing	14	58.3	10	41.7
Dependency Status	Indeterminate status	183	51.3	174	48.7
	Self-supporting	100	64.1	56	35.9
	Dependent	210	73.4	76	26.6
High School GPA	A	3	60.0	2	40.0
	B	15	57.7	11	42.3
	C or Less	42	49.4	43	50.6
	Missing	433	63.4	250	36.6
High School Diploma	Honors	5	41.7	7	58.3
	Core 40	36	50.7	35	49.3
	Regular or Missing	452	63.1	264	36.9
Major in Fall 2002	Humanities	9	40.9	13	59.1
	Science and Math	15	57.7	11	42.3
	Social Science	28	58.3	20	41.7
	Health	109	65.7	57	34.3

Business	58	64.4	32	35.6
Education	46	63.0	27	37.0
Computer	4	50.0	4	50.0
Engineering			1	100.0
Others	60	57.7	44	42.3
Undecided	164	62.8	97	37.2
College GPA				
A	108	78.3	30	21.7
B	245	76.8	74	23.2
C or Less	140	43.6	181	56.4
Missing			21	100.0
Remedial Coursework				
Remedial Math only	161	66.5	81	33.5
Remedial Language Arts only	18	62.1	11	37.9
Remedial Math and Language Arts	32	84.2	6	15.8
No Remedial Coursework	282	57.6	208	42.4
Full-time Enrollment in Fall 2002				
Part-time	209	54.6	174	45.4
Full-time	284	68.3	132	31.7
Frequency of participation in Supplemental Instruction				
Not in an SI Course	379	59.8	255	40.2
Never had SI but in an SI course	74	66.7	37	33.3
SI one to three times	23	74.2	8	25.8
SI four or more times	17	73.9	6	26.1
Frequency of participation in tutoring				
Did not receive tutoring	426	59.7	288	40.3
One to three times	42	79.2	11	20.8
More than 3 times	25	78.1	7	21.9
Participated in a course offering supplemental instruction				
Not in an SI Course	379	59.8	255	40.2
Yes, in an SI course	114	69.1	51	30.9
Participation in a learning community				
Not in a learning community	401	58.5	284	41.5
In a learning community	92	80.7	22	19.3
Aid/income status				
No financial aid	174	50.1	173	49.9
Other aid recipient, including loans	169	74.4	58	25.6
Other need-based grant recipient	7	63.6	4	36.4
Pell recipient	143	66.8	71	33.2
Total	493	61.7	306	38.3

Table 6.4. Logistic Regression Analysis of Persistence of Fall to Spring Semester in 2002 by First-Year Students at Region University

		Model 1		Model 2	
		Odds Ratio	*Sig.*	*Odds Ratio*	*Sig.*
Age	Age 21–24	0.364	***	0.398	***
	Age 25–29	0.325	***	0.345	**
	Age 30 and over	0.487	*	0.500	*
Gender	Male	1.076		1.080	
Ethnicity	Minority	0.583		0.591	
	Missing	1.490		1.620	
Dependency Status	Indeterminate status	0.662		0.713	
	Dependent	0.922		0.955	
High School GPA	B	2.762		2.948	
	Missing	2.072		2.311	
High School Diploma	Honors	0.368		0.479	
	Core 40	1.315		1.626	
Major in Fall 2002	Humanities	0.529		0.504	
	Science and Math	0.859		0.987	
	Social Science	0.806		0.858	
	Health	1.201		1.451	
	Business	1.571		1.536	

		Model 1		Model 2	
	Education	0.919		0.801	
	Computer	1.009		0.986	
	Others	1.006		1.085	
College GPA	A	2.048	*	2.146	*
	C or Less	0.345	***	0.357	***
Remedial Coursework	Remedial Math only	1.523	*	1.436	
	Remedial Language Arts only	1.140		1.188	
	Remedial Math and Language Arts	4.888	***	5.249	***
Enrollment in Fall 2002	Full Time	1.413	*	1.186	
Aid/income Status	Other aid recipient, including loans	2.229	***	2.219	***
	Other need-based grant recipient	1.432		1.629	
	Pell recipient	1.742	*	1.710	*
Frequency of Participation in Supplemental Instruction	Never had SI but in SI course			1.356	
	SI 1 to 3 times			1.129	
	SI 4 or more times			1.938	
Frequency of Participation in Tutoring	One to three times			2.375	*
	More than 3 times			1.717	
Participation in a Learning Community	Yes, participated			2.687	***
Number of Cases		799		799	
Model χ^2		166.943		185.746	
Nagelkerke R^2		0.256		0.282	
% Correctly Predicted		71.1%		71.7%	

Note: *** $p < 0.001$, ** $p < 0.01$, * $p < 0.05$

needed academic support in a particular area of their courses. There was not a significant difference between students who perceived themselves to have a high need for academic support and frequently sought out tutoring (more than three times) and those who did not perceive the need for tutoring. Again, the lack of a significance difference in persistence here may be practically important, because these students experienced college as more challenging but persisted nevertheless.

The only significant student demographic variable for this group was student age. Students over age twenty-one persisted at a lower rate than students under age twenty-one. Students in the twenty-five to twenty-nine-year-old age range had the lowest odds ratio when compared to traditional-age students. Students receiving Pell grants—the most substantial aid—and students who receive aid in the form of loans and other nongrant aid were more likely to persist than students not receiving aid.

Even with the academic support services, college grades were a strong predictor of student persistence. Students with A grades in college were more likely to persist than students with B grades, who were more likely to persist than students with C or lower grades. Generally, students in developmental coursework did not have significantly different odds of persistence than students who did not need developmental coursework, controlling for the other variables in the model, including a measure of academic preparation (high school diploma type). The exception was that students taking both developmental math and language arts courses were more likely to persist, suggesting that this coursework is having its intended impact on those students who need it.

This model explains only an estimated 28 percent of the variance in student persistence, suggesting there is much left still to be explained. Yet this does not diminish the important positive significance of the learning communities and tutoring at RU.

While this model controls for a number of individual differences, such as academic preparation and student demographics, a supplemental analysis to test for bias in who participates in the learning communities is still needed. It may be that more sophisticated students choose to participate. Alternatively, one administrator noted that first-generation students are advised to participate for the additional support. This type of statistical control for self-selection into campus programs is relatively new to higher education research, yet as methodology advances, IR practice must follow.

Evaluating the Evaluation

This example illustrates how evaluation can integrate with the inquiry cycle in two distinct ways. Early in the process, evaluation can be used in a truncated cycle in which the inquiry process jumps from assessment right to evaluation of a particular campus program. Even more important is when evaluation is integrated into a pilot test of a campus intervention and provides the campus team with feedback to complete the inquiry cycle. In these situations, evaluation usually becomes the assessment to begin the cycle again. If campuses have selected complex, resistant challenges—as a number of our partner campuses have—frequently, one expedition through the inquiry cycle leaves at least part of the challenge unanswered.

This evaluation approach meets the standards of rigor advocated by Patton, Morelon, Whitehead, and Hossler in Chapter One of this volume, who stated that "High-quality articles typically included most of the following attributes: they yielded statistically significant results or provided strong qualitative findings, they included large sample sizes, they included some form of a control group, and they contained detailed information about the retention-centered program." The regression of learning communities for RU yielded statistically significant results, but the sample size of about eight hundred students may have been a little small for the number of variables in the model. On larger campuses or when smaller campuses can use multiple grade levels (this was limited to first-year students), sample size would not be a problem. In this analysis, students who did not participate in learning communities formed the control group, along with controls from the other variables in the model for student demographic differences. A simultaneous equation analysis testing for self-selection difference between participants and nonparticipants and testing for the relationship to persistence would have been an even better analysis but would likely find similar results. Because evaluation and action inquiry are the theme of this chapter, the description of the retention program is intentionally limited here, but this is easily adjusted, and the description would need to be expanded for another audience.

The use of regression analysis had a clearly defined critical success indicator: student persistence from the first to the second semester. Future analyses will track the program impact into the second year or later years as data become available. The evaluation had clearly defined but easy-to-collect measures of program participation in several campus programs. Although the primary audience for this analysis was the campus team for their use in the inquiry process, the analysis could easily be shared with senior administration and is being shared with the funding agency that provided support to initiate the program. This type of rigorous analysis would also be beneficial beyond the campus and is of a scholarly caliber for publication in practitioner journals. The analytic rigor of the multivariate model used here is beyond that of most of the campus studies examined by Braxton, McKinney, and Reynolds in Chapter Two of this volume.

Conclusions

It is my hope that the example illustrates several key points. Rigorous evaluation is possible with extant institutional data with minimal additional data collection. In this example all variables except program participation data were already collected in regular institutional practice. In the instance of learning communities, registrar records provided participation data. For supplemental instruction and tutoring, participation was collected at the service site.

Chapter One of this volume ends with the questions, "How do institutions of higher education know that the programs and services that they offer contribute to undergraduate student retention? How do we know that the countless dollars and budgets that are labeled for retention efforts actually work?" Evaluation that is integrated with program pilot testing and that is academically rigorous, as suggested here, can provide administrators with the actionable knowledge to make difficult budgetary and programmatic decisions. Evaluation as an integral part of an inquiry process provides the evidence needed throughout the assessment, inquiry, and program development process as well as the final evidence to determine whether the program was effective and the challenge was met. The evaluation example here is illustrative, not the only way a campus could use evaluation in inquiry. Clearly, in some instances, qualitative evidence is necessary because of low numbers of students or to tease out the reasons a program is or is not working. Qualitative and quantitative data are a part of inquiry. More important than method is the integration of evaluation and evidence in program development and the integration of IR staff into institutional planning with campus administrators.

References

Hu, S., and St. John, E. P. "Student Persistence in a Public Higher Education System: Understanding Racial/Ethnic Differences." *The Journal of Higher Education,* 2001, 72(3), 265–286.

St. John, E. P. "Workable Models for Institutional Research on the Impact of Student Financial Aid." *Journal of Student Financial Aid,* 1992, 22(3), 13–26.

St. John, E. P. "Evaluating State Grant Programs: A Study of the Washington State Grant Programs." *Research in Higher Education,* 1999, 40(2), 149–170.

St. John, E. P., Hu, S., and Weber, J. "Keeping Public Colleges Affordable: A Study of Persistence in Indiana's Public Colleges and Universities." *Journal of Student Financial Aid,* 2000, 30(1), 21–32.

St. John, E. P., Hu, S., and Weber, J. "State Policy and the Affordability of Public Higher Education: The Influence of State Grants on Persistence in Indiana." *Research in Higher Education,* 2001, 42, 401–428.

St. John, E. P., Simmons, A. B., and Musoba, G. D. "Merit-Aware Admissions in Public Universities: Increasing Diversity." *Thought and Action,* 2002, 17(2), 35–46.

Somers, P., and St. John, E. P. "Interpreting Price Response in Enrollment Decisions: A Comparative Institutional Study." *Journal of Student Financial Aid,* 1997, 27(3), 15–36.

Somers, P., Woodhouse, S., and Cofer, J. "Pushing the Boulder Uphill: The Persistence of First-Generation College Students." *NASPA Journal,* 2004, 41, 418–435.

GLENDA DROOGSMA MUSOBA *is assistant professor of education at Florida International University. Previously she was policy analyst and associate director of the Indiana Project on Academic Success at Indiana University. She has a Ph.D. in higher education from Indiana University. Her research interests include higher education access and equity, persistence in higher education, education policy, K-16 education reform, and social justice.*

NEW DIRECTIONS FOR INSTITUTIONAL RESEARCH • DOI: 10.1002/ir

7

Although the process of integrating institutional research into professional practice is still in a formative stage, we have learned some lessons from our experience.

Lessons Learned: Institutional Research as Support for Academic Improvement

Edward P. St. John

As Patton, Morelon, Whitehead, and Hossler showed in Chapter One of this volume, there is, unfortunately, relatively little rigorous research that can inform institutions about best practices in student enrollment and persistence. Although at first this notion may seem counterintuitive, given the substantial volumes of work on educational attainment (Pascarella and Terenzini, 1991, 2005), the void seems traceable to the substantial valuation of traditional persistence models that have not provided a basis for evaluative research, as is evident in reviews of prior research in Chapters One and Three of this volume. Higher education research has been theoretically elegant and statistically sophisticated—providing information on the roles of students' academic and social engagement as intermediate outcomes—but has not adequately responded to the new challenge for public accountability. In particular, there is a need for evaluation of strategies for improvement processes within and across disciplines.

One way of viewing accountability in higher education is to consider accountability schemes that report descriptive statistics on persistence and other outcomes (Zumeta, 2001), but this approach favors institutions that have high persistence rates rather than encouraging and rewarding campuses that attract high-achieving students. Indeed, there is evidence that there are financial advantages for research universities in states with accountability systems (Weerts, 2002). An alternative is to work with common data systems

NEW DIRECTIONS FOR INSTITUTIONAL RESEARCH, no. 130, Summer 2006 © Wiley Periodicals, Inc.
Published online in Wiley InterScience (www.interscience.wiley.com) • DOI: 10.1002/ir.182

to identify and address challenges facing students and institutions. Evaluative research is needed that examines the impact of academic interventions, controlling for the preparation of students, which means, at a minimum, sound inferential statistical models. The goal of conducting research that can inform practice is not out of reach if we can learn the necessary lessons about standards, theory, and practice—the topics addressed in this volume. As a conclusion, I summarize lessons learned from these chapters, supplemented by other recent literature.

Standards for Research

With the growing emphasis on government accountability in education, it is important to consider the standards used for research on access, persistence, and other outcomes related to student success and educational attainment. Most of the education research used to build rationales for the education standards movement has focused on correlations between high school courses and subsequent outcomes (Becker, 2004; Heller, 2004) but has failed to consider the direct effects of education policies rationalized on this research. School reforms, accountability standards, and new graduation requirements have been rationalized on such research, but the limited research on the effects of such policies does not support claims about the efficacy of these policies. Rather, most of the K–12 reforms are positively associated with improvement in test scores (Hanushek and Raymond, 2004) but are negatively associated with high school graduation rates (St. John, Musoba, and Chung, 2004).

One possible way to avoid this accountability trap in higher education involves using research to inform improvement efforts within colleges and universities as a means of building cooperation with state agencies. In this approach, it is crucial that administrators and faculty members in the practitioner community, in collaboration with institutional researchers, engage in a serious and dedicated process of research-informed reform. The time commitments required to use this approach may make it difficult to use research-informed change as a universal accountability method. Nonetheless, such an approach merits exploration and further testing.

Even if politics does prevail and new accountability schemes are implemented, it will be important to break down barriers to educational opportunity and to experiment with new approaches to improving outcomes. Thus, whatever position one takes on the future of government accountability schemes in higher education, there is reason to reconsider the role of research. Research-informed improvement efforts may be workable within state systems that have accountability schemes linked to public funding, just as they may provide means of fending off top-down accountability. As difficult as research-informed change has proven to be, it may have merit in states that collect student-record data, regardless of the status of accountability.

But what standards should education and policy research meet before it can and should be used as a basis for government and institutional decisions about education improvement and finance? The chapters in this volume move a considerable distance toward answering this question. Three lessons emerge as paramount.

Lesson 1: Setting a Minimum Standard for Inferential Research. The minimum standard for inferential research on access and persistence requires sound theoretical foundations and the use of multivariate statistical models that control for the primary independent variables necessary to assess the effects of interventions (in other words, public finance policies or institutional interventions) on attainment outcomes.

The national and state reviews of prior evaluation research revealed that most research does not meet a generally accepted standard for inferential research. In Chapter One of this volume, Patton and colleagues revealed that, while there is extensive persistence research, there have been few studies that actually evaluate interventions based on theory-driven research. In Chapter Two, Braxton, McKinney, and Reynolds took a more in-depth look at evaluation studies that had been conducted previously in Indiana. They found that most studies were descriptive and that few had met a generally accepted standard for inferential research.

Descriptive information about differences in rates does not meet a minimum threshold for evaluation for two reasons: it does not control for other variables that influence the intended outcomes, and it does not control for selection (institutional or self-selection) in the analysis of effects. This standard meets one aspect of the goal: controlling the influence of other variables. The fact that so much of the evaluation research in higher education fails to meet even a minimum standard for inferential research reveals that institutions do not have adequate evaluative information for institutional decisions about educational improvement.

Lesson 2: The Need for Solid Design. To make causal inferences about interventions (public finance policies or institutional interventions) it is necessary to use experimental designs with random assignment or to test and control for selection effects.

Research that meets the inferential standard has generally been considered acceptable for higher education research and provides a reasonable basis for institutional decisions. However, most research on the effects of programs on students in higher education fails to control for selection—institutional decisions about eligibility and student self-selection decisions—so they stop short of providing causal information about interventions even when they examine direct and indirect effects. This newer standard for determining causal effects of intervention is now a federal requirement in education research (No Child Left Behind Act, 2001) and is crucial for research on educational attainment (Becker, 2004).

The random assignment of students and faculty into treatment and control groups may be desirable from an empirical vantage point, but frequently it is not possible in higher education, given the preference for student freedom to choose and faculty freedom to teach. Nevertheless, this higher standard poses a challenge for researchers in higher education as to how to address methodological issues related to selection. When an inferential standard is met and a variable for an intervention is significant in a logically sound model, we can be confident that involvement in the intervention made a difference, but we do not know if the difference was caused by selection (for example, students choosing to participate) or by the intervention itself. Higher education researchers such as DesJardins (2005) are engaged in testing the use of instrument variables to control for selection (by institutions or as self-selection by students), regression discontinuity analysis, and other methods for untangling questions related to selection.

Given the state of knowledge, it is important to check whether or not involvement in interventions is random if inferential models are used. In Chapter Six of this volume, Musoba recognized this limitation. The state of the art in attainment research is in transition due to higher expectations of educational research and the use of statistical methods in sociology and education, and it will be necessary to make adjustments in evaluation research as well.

Lesson 3: The Benefits of Qualitative Research.   Qualitative research on enrollment, persistence, and other attainment outcomes can enrich and illuminate understanding of linkages hypothesized by theoretical models, reveal critical challenges overlooked by theory, and provide explanations for the effects of public policies and institutional interventions.

In higher education, researchers cannot rely exclusively on empirical research methods. Given the array of accepted ways of knowing in academe, even the best quantitative research will be overlooked by many in academe. Ideally, both quantitative and qualitative methods should be used in research on educational outcomes. In this volume, Hansen and Borden (Chapter Four) and St. John, McKinney, and Tuttle (Chapter Five) describe how qualitative methods can be integrated into institutional research and used to inform change processes.

Institutional research as a field—like policy studies—must meet generally accepted empirical standards, given the nature of decision-making processes. However, qualitative studies are also needed to build understanding of challenges and effects of interventions. In fact, while empirical studies are needed to provide proof of effects, qualitative studies are often necessary to build an understanding of the reasons that interventions worked or failed as well as to reveal ways that practices might be altered to improve outcomes.

The Theory Problem Reconsidered

Theory plays a crucial role in research on educational attainment because it guides the selection of variables for statistical models, the assignment of individuals to treatment groups in random experiments (characteristics for selection), and the interpretation of results in both quantitative and qualitative research. Therefore, it is important that institutional researchers reconsider the role of theory, rather than select one theory because of its dominance in the literature over others. Three lessons emerge from this consideration.

Lesson 4: Theories of Persistence. While a substantial amount of persistence research uses generally accepted theory, there has been relatively little prior evaluation research on persistence interventions that meets a minimum standard for inferential research.

Theories of involvement and engagement dominate research on student persistence (Braxton, 2000; Hossler, Bean, and Associates, 1990; Pascarella and Terenzini, 2005). There are three major problems with using this theory as the primary basis for research that evaluates the effects of interventions and public policy on educational attainment.

First, as described in Chapters One and Two of this volume, this area of research has been used to rationalize interventions but has not been used to evaluate the effects of interventions rationalized on the basis of the theory. Since the theory focuses largely on involvement and engagement as measures of integration, it provides a basis for recommending involvement strategies, as discussed in Chapters One and Three of this volume, but does not provide a rationale for evaluating other types of interventions. For this task we need a better theory base for examining outcomes related to attainment.

Second, recent studies document that student engagement is influenced by family income and student aid (Hurtado, Nelson-Laird, and Perorarzio, 2004; Sedlacek and Sheu, 2004). The current work-loan burden after need-based grant aid is substantial—about $8,000 per year on average for student families earning less than $25,000 (Advisory Committee, 2002). It requires many hours of work to pay this annual bill, which reduces time for student involvement. Therefore, engagement theories require reformulation based on recent research on the role of finances. There may be a need to reconceptualize engagement theories of persistence to integrate an understanding of the role of family income and student aid in enabling student involvement. It is important to build on understandings from social and economic research rather than pursue a separate line of inquiry with limited relevance to policy or evaluation.

In spite of these limitations, our theories of persistence have provided a substantial contribution to the field of higher education. In particular, theory and research on student integration provide a lens through which to view student involvement in academic process, including interaction with faculty. For example, this body of work has influenced the emergence of learning communities. However, the task remains to evaluate these new models using balanced models that consider the roles and influence of social and economic background on student involvement. In addition, this area of theory could inform a new generation of work that examines problems specific to different academic fields, a crucial issue in the period ahead.

Lesson 5: Using a Sound Base of Social and Economic Theory. Research on the effects of interventions (public finance policies or institutional interventions) should consider social theory and research on attainment as well as economic theory and research in the design of models for examining enrollment, persistence, and other attainment-related outcomes.

To meet the standards for inferential or causal research on the impact of institutional interventions and public policies, it is necessary to use a sound theory base. The theories of fit integration and engagement widely used in higher education research are not adequate to this task when used as the primary theory base because they overlook the substantial role of inequalities in preparation for and involvement during college resulting from income inequalities. It is crucial to step back and consider social and economic theories when considering the roles of involvement or engagement, interventions, and financial aid.

Social theory has long focused on the role of family background—including parents' income—in the attainment process (Alexander and Eckland, 1978; Blau and Duncan, 1967). More recently, the concepts of social capital and cultural capital have been used as explanations for the role of social force. The cultural capital argument views the link between family culture and education attainment as central (Bourdieu, 1980), while social capital focuses on the role of networks and other mechanisms that are linked to opportunity (Coleman, 1988). Both theories have been widely used in higher education research on attainment processes. Regardless of the specific explanation used to interpret the role of social forces, it is important to consider these variables as foundational.

Economic theory, too, has been central to research on attainment process for decades, especially in research on college students. Human capital theory (Becker, 1964)—especially the argument that individuals and government consider the costs and benefits of investment in education—has been used in research on college students (see, for example, Jackson, 1978; Manski and Wise, 1983) and has been a major argument. More recent studies that establish linkages between finances (income and financial aid) and both preparation (St. John and others, 2004) and integration during college (Hurtado, Nelson-Laird, and Perorarzio, 2004; Sedlacek and Sheu, 2004) provide even more compelling evidence that the role of finances is integral to attainment.

Lesson 6: Using Existing Data. Institutional records on high school preparation, student aid, admissions, and student enrollment (that is, workable models) provide a basis for models that evaluate the effects of interventions on attainment outcomes, provided that information of involvement in interventions is also available.

Institutional record systems developed from data normally collected from schools, colleges, and other agencies provide an appropriate database for research on educational attainment. In the study summarized in Chapter Six of this volume, Musoba demonstrates that this approach can also be extended to the analysis of the effect of intervention programs. Although empirical studies are crucial for evaluation purposes, qualitative studies may be even more important as means of building understandings among practitioners, as discussed by Hansen and Borden in Chapter Four of this volume and by St. John, McKinney, and Tuttle in Chapter Five. Institutional researchers should use both methods in studies aimed at informing institutional change processes, as argued by Hansen and Borden and illustrated by other chapters in this volume.

Collaborations Between Researchers and Practitioners

In Chapter Four of this volume, Hansen and Borden challenge all of us to think about strategies for building collaboration between institutional researchers and practitioners in higher education (such as administrators and faculty) to address critical challenges. The Indiana Project for Academic Success (IPAS) used an action inquiry approach for both through assessment to identify critical challenges and through action inquiry to find new solutions for them. While IPAS is a work in progress, it is possible to learn from the experience to date.

Lesson 7: Academic Challenges Remain. Although substantial gains are apparently being made in retention during the first two years of college, there are also critical challenges related to persistence to degree completion. It is especially important to focus on building an understanding of academic success within and across academic fields, particularly for studies that consider how major choices—and even how performance in tough courses in those majors—influence persistence.

The academic disciplines are at the core of academic communities and form the basis for the academic programs in most institutions of higher education. Higher education research on college students has informed innovations in course delivery for first-year students, a type of intervention that is now being evaluated (as Musoba describes in Chapter Six of this volume), but that has stopped short of providing a basis for designing interventions within academic fields.

There are numerous academic challenges that merit attention. For example, the humanities disciplines have lost students in recent decades due in part to the low earnings of graduates in these fields (Bradburn and others, 2003). Historically, the humanities and liberal arts were thought to be preparation for professional employment. In this new context, perhaps these fields are preparation for graduate professional programs, an issue that merits consideration. Not only is there a need for innovations that link the humanities with the professions as part of undergraduate programs, but such interventions should probably be pilot tested and evaluated.

One major challenge is for institutional researchers and interested faculty to work together on addressing learning issues within their academic fields. This involves not only building pedagogical content knowledge within fields but also finding better ways to integrate information on student involvement in academic innovations with balanced models that control for student background. A new generation of innovation and research is needed to explore the academic pathways students travel to academic success.

Lesson 8: Using Workable Models. Workable models for enrollment, major choice, and persistence can be used to identify critical challenges as part of a systematic assessment process, including analyses within and across academic fields.

As described elsewhere in this volume, the assessment process used in IPAS involved examining extant databases to identify critical challenges. Analyses were conducted at the state level and for participating campuses. Statewide, it was evident that there were challenges for African American students with respect to academic integration, as measured by persistence in academic fields. In Chapter Three of this volume, Carter reviews the literature on persistence by African Americans and finds research on social integration and financial aid, but relatively little information on academic integration within major fields. Thus, a near void in the literature, echoing findings from the national review described in Chapter One, represents the challenge uncovered in the statewide assessment. Using extant data and sound theoretical models (in other words, workable models) can lead to the identification of challenges that face practitioners. However, the literature on best practices did not align well with many of the challenges facing campuses in Indiana.

This method can be adapted by college campuses, and institutional researchers can work directly with strategic planning groups to use institutional data to identify the critical challenges facing their campuses. At the very least, the workable models approach can supplement the assessment methods more common in higher education (see, for example, Banta and others, 2002). Literature reviews provide a further source of information about best practices, although the reviews presented in Chapters One, Two, and Three of this volume suggest a misalignment between challenges and these practices.

Lesson 9: Action Inquiry and Institutional Context. Using action inquiry can overcome the problem of solutions seeking problems (and the paradox in the notion of best practices) in efforts to address critical challenges.

Whether or not there is a sound literature on best practices as they relate to challenges revealed through research, it is important that decisions about strategies to be implemented be informed by an understanding of the institutional context. As discussed in Chapters Four and Five of this volume, action inquiry can be used toward this end.

The paradox in the notion of best practices is the implication that there is a set of practices or processes that should be universally used to improve outcomes, whereas matching interventions with contexts and evolving interventions within their contexts are essential to best practice. Scanning the literature to find practices that have worked in other contexts is only a starting point for action inquiry. For example, when features of the now-popular concept of linking a set of courses for a group of students in learning communities are adapted in commuter campuses, it is necessary to address differences in learning and living environments for both students and faculty. Using an inquiry-based approach can help a faculty working group decide whether and how to adapt this type of strategy.

The case examples in Chapter Five illustrate the inquiry process, which starts with building an understanding of why a problem exists in the first place. If a commuter campus has a persistence problem with first-year students, the campus may decide to try out the learning communities approach. However, if its students are mostly part time and are at greatest risk of not returning for their second fall term, then the campus might want to test the idea of using a set of connected courses that span three or more terms, rather than a one- or two-term approach. Understanding the problem—considering whether first- to second-term persistence or continuous enrollment is the problem during the first two or three years—is important to consider before identifying and selecting possible practices.

Lesson 10: Collaborations. Collaborations between researchers and practitioners can be used to inform the organizational change process.

Several of the chapters in this volume illustrate the importance of collaboration between researchers and practitioners. Hansen and Borden (Chapter Four) make a strong argument for such collaboration, a position that influenced the design of IPAS. The IPAS project experience further reflects the importance of collaboration, as a couple of examples illustrate.

Focus groups conducted by IPAS consultants have been an important part of the early inquiry process, providing a means of bringing students' voices into the process (see Chapter Five). In fact, we have found the focus groups generally seem more open when they are run by an independent researcher. When practitioners—faculty members or student affairs administrators—run focus groups in their own programs, discussions tend to be less frank and open, and positive comments are emphasized. If the role of the early stages of the inquiry process is to uncover the reasons that a challenge exists, then openness is crucial. Independent campus researchers may be able to provide this type of support for practitioners engaged in inquiry aimed at building an understanding of the challenges they face. Such a service can be provided by institutional research offices or by graduate students in higher education programs.

In addition, researchers should be involved in the design of interventions if the aim is to learn from them as pilot tests. In Chapter Six of this volume, Musoba describes the reasons for these linkages and gives an illustrative example from an evaluation. Involving researchers in the design of the interventions can make it easier to collect evaluative information during the intervention. Such a collaborative approach distinguishes pilot tests of the type proposed in Chapter Five from other innovations in practice. The limitation of innovation without a research component is that new understanding might not be shared beyond a very limited community of practice. Yet the problem with treating interventions as pilot tests is that it is a more labor-intensive process requiring the support of researchers.

NEW DIRECTIONS FOR INSTITUTIONAL RESEARCH • DOI: 10.1002/ir

Given the labor-intensive nature of the action inquiry process, it seems important to focus the process on the issues that are most crucial to improving student success. Not all adaptations to practice merit the time investment of extensive inquiry; in fact most do not. Therefore, it is crucial to select challenges as outcomes of the assessment process carefully, choosing topics that merit time and have a group of interested practitioners.

Lesson 11: Funding. Integrating evaluative research into strategic planning and budgeting processes within institutions continues to be a challenge.

In theory, planning and budgeting processes should be designed to use evaluative information in deliberations about policy decisions. In the IPAS project there have been a few early examples of campuses securing funding for the action inquiry process. For example, three of the campuses in the northwest corner of the state received funds to conduct surveys of working students, a collaboratively defined challenge area. Other campuses have provided release time for faculty who are engaged in the IPAS process. The IPAS project could not provide minigrants to participating campuses, so practitioner involvement was voluntary. Variability in involvement resulted, it seemed, from the local enthusiasm of practitioners and both the extent and quality of assistance provided (hypotheses that will be tested in a subsequent formative evaluation). However, one of the project aims is to inform institutional budgetary decisions. Involved practitioners often hoped to get funding for projects that proved successful. From a project-management perspective, there is still a question, too, whether campuses will invest in areas that could have promising results.

These questions are important from the perspective of funding agencies as well. Very often, funding is given for projects based on a hope that they will be sustained by the campuses after the project ends. In this case, the aim is to provide professional development and to test the notion of integrating research and practice in action inquiry to address critical challenges. It remains to be seen if this project will create a residual of learning and of using research-based inquiry to make institutional investment decisions. In other words, the IPAS project is an experiment with a new form of practice, and events will determine what can be learned.

Lesson 12: Using State Data Systems. State data systems can be used to inform improvement processes in higher education when the barriers to collaboration are removed.

The IPAS project has demonstrated that state databases can be used in systematic ways to promote improvement. The same process is possible within institutional systems, given that state data are collected from institutions in the first place. Colleges and universities can follow a similar process using institutional data but may lack some information on high school courses and transfer within the state system. The additional data from the state on high school courses, financial aid applications, and transfer made the use of state data more appealing in this case. Several states now have statewide databases that combine information on high school students, college students, and employment. Linking these databases to track students over time is important because it can help us to build an understanding of preparation, enrollment, choice of major, and employment outcomes. It may be desirable for other institutions and state agencies to collaborate on the use of data to inform innovations, using methods similar to those tested in Indiana.

There are many other potential uses of state databases to encourage academic reform. Most require the process of carefully linking data to track student progress over time. In states with large-scale data systems, it makes good sense to put them to use in support of institutional improvement. Our experience with the use of state data systems may encourage others to try out a similar process.

Conclusions

The early twenty-first century has been a period of rising public expectations for high school preparation and college attainment. Many states have taken steps toward increasing high school graduation requirements, and a few have put need-based grant programs in place to ensure opportunity for students who prepare. There are many remaining questions about whether these new policies will have their intended effects. However, colleges and universities are facing the challenge of how best to respond to the new mandate for expansion. Rather than wait and see how the new policies turn out, it is important that institutions of higher education position themselves to respond to the new challenges of expanding opportunity for a new generation of first-time students. This volume has taken a step forward in the debate about expanding opportunity by addressing three interrelated issues related to research on persistence and other attainment outcomes.

First, there are methodological issues facing institutional researchers and practitioners in higher education who are interested in creating more and better pathways to educational success. Many eloquent studies of persistence have been conducted, but there has been relatively little evaluative research on the interventions rationalized based on this research. Most of the research on best practices has not met a generally acceptable inferential statistical research standard—a standard that should be met to confirm that new practices have their intended effect. In addition, a higher research standard should be considered, one that involves testing for the effects of self-selection and official selection processes. In addition to meeting reasonable standards for statistical research, it is important to consider the role of qualitative inquiries in building an understanding of the challenges facing college faculty and student affairs practitioners who are on the front line in the efforts to respond to new educational challenges in higher education. Not only do qualitative studies bring students' voices into the change process, but they also help illuminate the problems in ways that make those problems more understandable for most practitioners, building a better base for collaboration.

Second, the goal of expanding college opportunities in the United States requires a rethinking of the theories used in research on student persistence. Most persistence theory is relatively silent about the role of financial inequalities, yet the most serious problem with research on student engagement and involvement may be that it largely overlooks the influence (that is, the work-loan burden after grants) of scarce family resources on hours worked, time for courses and faculty interaction, and opportunities for social engagement. However, even the use of cultural and social capital theories—concepts that illuminate the role of families—can overlook the role of finances unless studies are carefully crafted. Creating educational programs that meet the educational needs of working students represents an especially critical challenge in higher education, given the problems with financial access.

Third, the process of addressing basic challenges related to expanding and improving educational opportunity necessarily requires collaboration between researchers and practitioners. To address these new challenges will require more than applying known practices thought to be "the best" because they are aligned with theory or because they have worked with traditional college students. Rather, responding to the learning needs of new first-generation students will mean pioneering new educational pathways. In this volume, we present some preliminary evidence related to the use of action inquiry to address critical challenges. This approach holds some promise, but there is a great deal more to be learned.

References

Advisory Committee on Student Financial Assistance. *Empty Promises: The Myth of College Access in America.* Washington, D.C.: Advisory Committee on Student Financial Assistance, 2002.

Alexander, K. L., and Eckland, B. K. "Basic Attainment Processes: A Replication and Extension, 1999." *Sociology of Education,* 1978, *48*(4), 457–495.

Banta, T. W., and Associates. *Building a Scholarship of Assessment.* San Francisco: Jossey-Bass, 2002.

Becker, G. S. *Human Capital: A Theoretical and Empirical Analysis with Special Reference to Education.* New York: Columbia University Press, 1964.

Becker, W. E. "Omitted Variables and Sample Selection in Studies of College-Going Decisions." In E. P. St. John (ed.), *Readings on Equal Education.* Vol. 19: *Public Policy and College Access: Investigating the Federal and State Roles in Equalizing Postsecondary Opportunity.* New York: AMS Press, 2004.

Blau, P. M., and Duncan, O. D. *The American Occupational Structure.* New York: Wiley, 1967.

Bourdieu, P. *The Logic of Practice* (R. Nice, trans.). Stanford, Calif.: Stanford University Press, 1980.

Bradburn, E. M., and others. *Baccalaureate and Beyond: A Descriptive Summary of 1999–2000 Bachelor's Degree Recipients, One Year Later—with an Analysis of Time to Degree.* NCES no. 2003–165. Washington, D.C.: National Center for Education Statistics, 2003.

Braxton, J. M. "Reinvigorating Theory and Research on the Departure Puzzle." In J. M. Braxton (ed.), *Reworking the Student Departure Puzzle.* Nashville, Tenn.: Vanderbilt University Press, 2000.

Coleman, J. C. "Social Capital in the Creation of Human Capital." *American Journal of Sociology,* 1988, *94,* S95–S120.

DesJardins, S. L. *Investigating the Efficacy of Using Selection Modeling in Research of the Gates Millennium Scholars Program.* Presented to the Gates Millennium Scholars Research Advisory Council, 2005.

Hanushek, E. A., and Raymond, M. E. "Does School Accountability Lead to Improved Student Performance?" Working Paper 10591. Cambridge, Mass.: National Bureau of Economic Research, 2004.

Heller, D. E. "NCES Research on College Participation: A Critical Analysis." In E. P. St. John (ed.), *Readings on Equal Education.* Vol. 19: *Public Policy and College Access: Investigating the Federal and State Roles in Equalizing Postsecondary Opportunity.* New York: AMS Press, 2004.

Hossler, D., Bean, J. P., and Associates. *The Strategic Management of College Enrollment.* San Francisco: Jossey-Bass, 1990.

Hurtado, S., Nelson-Laird, T. F., and Perorarzio, T. E. "The Transition to College for Low-Income Students: The Impact of the GMS Program." In E. P. St. John (ed.), *Readings on Equal Education.* Vol. 20: *Improving Access and College Success for Diverse Students: Studies of the Gates Millennium Scholars Program.* New York: AMS Press, 2004.

Jackson, G. A. "Financial Aid and Student Enrollment." *The Journal of Higher Education,* 1978, *49,* 548–574.

Manski, C. F., and Wise, D. A. *College Choice in America.* Cambridge, Mass.: Harvard University Press, 1983.

No Child Left Behind Act of 2001, Public Law 107–110.

Pascarella, E. T., and Terenzini, P. T. *How College Affects Students: Findings and Insights from Twenty Years of Research.* San Francisco: Jossey-Bass, 1991.

Pascarella, E. T., and Terenzini, P. T. *How College Affects Students: Vol. 2. A Third Decade of Research.* San Francisco: Jossey-Bass, 2005.

St. John, E. P., Musoba, G. D., and Chung, C. G. "Academic Access: The Impact of State Education Policies." In E. P. St. John (ed.), *Readings on Equal Education.* Vol. 19: *Public Policy and College Access: Investigating the Federal and State Roles in Equalizing Postsecondary Opportunity.* New York: AMS Press, 2004.

St. John, E. P., and others. "Meeting the Access Challenge: An Examination of Indiana's Twenty-First Century Scholars Program." *Research in Higher Education,* 2004, *45*(8), 829–873.

Sedlacek, W. E., and Sheu, H. B. "Correlates of Leadership Activities of Gates Millennium Scholars." In E. P. St. John (ed.), *Readings on Equal Education.* Vol. 20: *Improving Access and College Success for Diverse Students: Studies of the Gates Millennium Scholars Program.* New York: AMS Press, 2004.

Weerts, D. J. *State Governments and Research Universities: A Framework for a Renewal Partnership.* New York: Routledge, 2002.

Zumeta, W. "Public Policy and Accountability in Higher Education: Lessons from the Past and Present for the New Millennium." In D. E. Heller (ed.), *The States and Public Higher Education Policy: Affordability, Access and Accountability.* Baltimore: Johns Hopkins University Press, 2001.

EDWARD P. ST. JOHN *is Algo D. Henderson Collegiate Professor of Education at the Center for the Study of Higher and Postsecondary Education at the University of Michigan. His research focuses on educational policy and public finance in both K-12 and higher education.*

INDEX

AAC&U. *See* Association of American Colleges and Universities (AAC&U)
Academic program improvement: institutional research as support for, 95–106; using action research to support, 47–61
Academic success, refocusing on, 3–6
ACE. *See* American Council on Education
Action inquiry, 102–103; case examples, 70; and examples of evaluation loop, 70–71; and inquiry to action, 73–75; introducing, 66; and multicampus collaborations, 72–73; at partner campuses, 69; situating, 63–66; and using full inquiry cycle, 72; using, to address critical challenges, 63–75
Action research model: applications of, 50–57; applying to higher education reform, 59–60; contrasted with traditional institutional research approach, 51 *Tab.* 4.1; definition of, 49–50; implications, 60–61; overcoming barriers to implementing, 58–59; possible barriers to, 57–58; using, to support academic program improvement, 47–61
Advisory Committee on Student Financial Assistance, 41, 99
African Americans, 5, 33–43
Ahlburg, D. A., 33
Alaska Natives, 37
Alexander, K. L., 100
Allen, W. R., 33, 38–40, 65
Allen-Haynes, L., 3
American Council on Education (ACE), 41
Andreu, M. L., 9
Argyris, C., 48
Ashford, S. J., 59
Asker, E. H., 6
Association of American Colleges and Universities (AAC&U), 59
Astin, A. W., 14, 17, 40
Attinasi, L. C., 9
Avalos, J., 40

Backer, R., 19
Baker, S., 15

Baker, T. L., 42
Balderston, F. E., 63, 64
Ball, S. R., 9
Banta, T. W., 65, 102
Barker, R. T., 48, 49
Barker, S. B., 48, 49
Bean, J. P., 9, 37, 99
Becker, G. S., 100
Becker, W. E., 96, 97
Bennett, J. B., 59
Bepko, G., 54
Berger, J. B., 9, 40, 41
Berry, T. R., 12
Bifulco, R., 11
Black, L. C., 9
Blackwell, J. M., 36
Blau, P. M., 100
Bonous-Hammarth, M., 38, 40
Borden, V.M.H., 3, 47, 74, 78, 101
Boudreau, C., 40
Bourdieu, P., 100
Boyd, V., 19
Bradburn, E. M., 101
Brain drain syndrome, 25
Braxton, J. M., 1, 2, 6, 9, 25, 28, 31, 32, 34, 37, 77, 79, 93, 97, 99
Brier, E. M., 28
Brotherson, M. J., 48
Bynum, J. E., 40

Cabrera, A. F., 9, 42
Carr, A., 60
Carter, D. F., 3, 5, 9, 33, 34, 40, 41, 64, 102
Chaffee, E. E., 64
Cheit, E. F., 64
Chung, C. G., 5, 34, 65, 96
Clayton-Pederson, A. R., 40
Coch, L., 47
Cofer, J., 78
Coleman, J. C., 100
Colton, C., 17
Colton, G., 17
Columbia University, 48
Context, institutional, 102–103
Coordinated Studies Program (CSP), 15, 16
Core 40, 26
Corey, S., 48

Back Issue/Subscription Order Form

Copy or detach and send to:

Jossey-Bass, A Wiley Imprint, 989 Market Street, San Francisco CA 94103-1741

Call or fax toll-free: Phone 888-378-2537 6:30AM – 3PM PST; Fax 888-481-2665

Back Issues: Please send me the following issues at $29 each
(Important: please include ISBN number for each issue.)

_____

_____

_____

$ _____   Total for single issues

$ _____   SHIPPING CHARGES: SURFACE   Domestic Canadian
                                                First Item $5.00 $6.00
                                                Each Add'l Item $3.00 $1.50
                        For next-day and second-day delivery rates, call the number listed above.

Subscriptions   Please __ start __ renew my subscription to *New Directions for Institutional Research* for the year 2_____ at the following rate:

U.S.	__ Individual $80	__ Institutional $170
Canada	__ Individual $80	__ Institutional $210
All Others	__ Individual $104	__ Institutional $244

Online subscriptions are available via Wiley InterScience!

**For more information about online subscriptions visit
www.wileyinterscience.com**

$ _____   Total single issues and subscriptions (Add appropriate sales tax for your state for single issue orders. No sales tax for U.S. subscriptions. Canadian residents, add GST for subscriptions and single issues.)

__Payment enclosed (U.S. check or money order only)

__VISA __ MC __ AmEx # _____ Exp. Date _____

Signature _____ Day Phone _____

__ Bill Me (U.S. institutional orders only. Purchase order required.)

Purchase order # _____
                    Federal Tax ID13559302   GST 89102 8052

Name _____

Address _____

_____

Phone _____ E-mail _____

For more information about Jossey-Bass, visit our Web site at www.josseybass.com

OTHER TITLES AVAILABLE IN THE
NEW DIRECTIONS FOR INSTITUTIONAL RESEARCH SERIES
Robert K. Toutkoushian, Editor-in-Chief

IR129   **Analyzing Faculty Work and Rewards: Using Boyer's Four Domains of Scholarship**
John M. Braxton
Boyer's four domains—scholarships of discovery, application, integration, and teaching—influence and define scholars as their professional roles, career stages, and research goals change. This volume offers practical suggestions for academic reward structure, graduate school preparation, and state policy.
ISBN: 0-7879-8674-7

IR128   **Workforce Development and Higher Education: A Strategic Role for Institutional Research**
Richard A. Voorhees, Lee Harvey
Workforce development is a growing area for higher education. This volume examines its conceptual underpinnings from an international perspective, and it provides practical institutional case studies and specific techniques for gauging the market potential for new instructional programs. It discusses suggested projects and studies for IR personnel to consider on their campuses.
ISBN: 0-7879-8365-9

IR127   **Survey Research: Emerging Issues**
Paul D. Umbach
Demands for accountability are forcing colleges and universities to conduct more high-quality surveys to gauge institutional effectiveness. New technologies are improving survey implementation as well as researchers' ability to effectively analyze data. This volume examines these emerging issues in a rapidly changing environment and highlights lessons learned from past research.
ISBN: 0-7879-8329-2

IR126   **Enhancing Alumni Research: European and American Perspectives**
David J. Weerts, Javier Vidal
The increasing globalization of higher education has made it easy to compare problems, goals, and tools associated with conducting alumni research worldwide. This research is also being used to learn about the impact, purposes, and successes of higher education. This volume will help institutional leaders use alumni research to respond to the increasing demands of state officials, accrediting agencies, employers, prospective students, parents, and the general public.
ISBN: 0-7879-8228-8

IR125   **Minority Retention: What Works?**
Gerald H. Gaither
Examines some of the best policies, practices, and procedures to achieve greater diversity and access, while controlling costs and maintaining quality. Looks at institutions that are majority-serving, tribal, Hispanic-serving, and historically black. Emphasizes that the key to retention is in the professional commitment of faculty and staff to student-centered efforts, and includes practical ideas adaptable to different institutional goals.
ISBN: 0-7879-7974-0

IR124   **Unique Campus Contexts: Insights for Research and Assessment**
Jason E. Lane, M. Christopher Brown II
Summarizes what we know about professional schools, transnational campuses, proprietary schools, religious institutions, and corporate universities. As more students take advantage of these specialized educational environments, conducting meaningful research becomes a challenge. The authors argue for the importance of educational context and debunk the one-size-fits-all approach to assessment, evaluation, and research. Effective institutional measures of inquiry, benchmarks, and indicators must be congruent with the mission, population, and function of each unique campus context.
ISBN: 0-7879-7973-2

IR123   **Successful Strategic Planning**
Michael J. Dooris, John M. Kelley, James F. Trainer
Explains the value of strategic planning in higher education to improve conditions and meet missions (hiring better faculty, recruiting stronger students, upgrading facilities, improving programs, acquiring resources), and what planning tools and methodologies have been used at various campuses. Goes beyond the activity of planning to investigate successful ways to implement and infuse strategic plans throughout the organization. Case studies from various campuses show different ways to achieve success.
ISBN: 0-7879-7792-6

IR122   **Assessing Character Outcomes in College**
Jon C. Dalton, Terrence R. Russell, Sally Kline
Examines several perspectives on the role of higher education in developing students' character, and illustrates approaches to defining and assessing character outcomes. Moral, civic, ethical, and spiritual development are key aspects of students' growth and experience in college, so how can educators encourage good values and assess their impact?
ISBN: 0-7879-7791-8

IR121   **Overcoming Survey Research Problems**
Stephen R. Porter
As demand for survey research has increased, survey response rates have decreased. This volume examines an array of survey research problems and best practices, from both the literature and field practitioners, to provide solutions to increase response rates while controlling costs. Discusses administering longitudinal studies, doing surveys on sensitive topics such as student drug and alcohol use, and using new technologies for survey administration.
ISBN: 0-7879-7477-3

IR120   **Using Geographic Information Systems in Institutional Research**
Daniel Teodorescu
Exploring the potential of geographic information systems (GIS) applications in higher education administration, this issue introduces IR professionals and campus administrators to a powerful presentation and analysis tool. Chapters explore the benefits of working with the spatial component of data in recruitment, admissions, facilities, alumni development, and other areas, with examples of actual GIS applications from several higher education institutions.
ISBN: 0-7879-7281-9

IR119   **Maximizing Revenue in Higher Education**
F. King Alexander, Ronald G. Ehrenberg
This volume presents edited versions of some of the best articles from a forum
on institutional revenue generation sponsored by the Cornell Higher Education
Research Institute. The chapters provide different perspectives on revenue
generation and how institutions are struggling to find an appropriate balance
between meeting public expectations and maximizing private market forces.
The insights provided about options and alternatives will enable campus
leaders, institutional researchers, and policymakers to better understand
evolving patterns in public and private revenue reliance.
ISBN: 0-7879-7221-5

IR118   **Studying Diverse Institutions: Contexts, Challenges, and Considerations**
M. Christopher Brown II, Jason E. Lane
This volume examines the contextual and methodological issues pertaining to
studying diverse institutions (including women's colleges, tribal colleges, and
military academies), and provides effective and useful approaches for higher
education administrators, institutional researchers and planners, policymakers,
and faculty seeking to better understand students in postsecondary education.
It also offers guidelines to asking the right research questions, employing the
appropriate research design and methods, and analyzing the data with respect
to the unique institutional contexts.
ISBN: 0-7879-6990-7

IR117   **Unresolved Issues in Conducting Salary-Equity Studies**
Robert K. Toutkoushian
Chapters discuss the issues surrounding how to use faculty rank, seniority, and
experience as control variables in salary-equity studies. Contributors review the
challenges of conducting a salary-equity study for nonfaculty administrators
and staff—who constitute the majority of employees, even in academic
institutions—and examine the advantages and disadvantages of using
hierarchical linear modeling to measure pay equity. They present a case-study
approach to illustrate the political and practical challenges that researchers
often face when conducting a salary-equity study for an institution. This is a
companion volume to Conducting Salary-Equity Studies: Alternative
Approaches to Research (IR115).
ISBN: 0-7879-6863-3

IR116   **Reporting Higher Education Results: Missing Links in the Performance
Chain**
Joseph C. Burke, Henrick P. Minassians
The authors review performance reporting's coverage, content, and customers,
they examine in depth the reporting indicators, types, and policy concerns,
and they compare them among different states' reports. They highlight
weaknesses in our current performance reporting—such as a lack of
comparable indicators for assessing the quality of undergraduate education—
and make recommendations about how to best use and improve performance
information.
ISBN: 0-7879-6336-4

IR115   **Conducting Salary-Equity Studies: Alternative Approaches to Research**
Robert K. Toutkoushian
Synthesizing nearly 30 years of research on salary equity from the field of
economics and the experiences of past studies, this issue launches an important
dialogue between scholars and institutional researchers on the methodology

and application of salary-equity studies in today's higher education institutions. The first of a two-volume set on the subject, it also bridges the gap between academic research and the more pragmatic statistical and political considerations in real-life institutional salary studies.
ISBN: 0-7879-6335-6

IR114 **Evaluating Faculty Performance**
Carol L. Colbeck
This issue brings new insights to faculty work and its assessment in light of reconsideration of faculty work roles, rapid technological change, increasing bureaucratization of the core work of higher education, and public accountability for performance. Exploring successful methods that individuals, institutions, and promotion and tenure committees are using for evaluations of faculty performance for career development, this issue is an indispensable guide to academic administrators and institutional researchers involved in the faculty evaluation process.
ISBN: 0-7879-6334-8

IR113 **Knowledge Management: Building a Competitive Advantage in Higher Education**
Andreea M. Serban, Jing Luan
Provides a comprehensive discussion of knowledge management, covering its theoretical, practical, and technological aspects with an emphasis on their relevance for applications in institutional research. Chapters examine the theoretical basis and impact of data mining; discuss the role of institutional research in customer relationship management; and provide a framework for the integration of institutional research within the larger context of organization learning. With a synopsis of technologies that support knowledge management and an exploration of future developments in this field, this volume assists institutional researchers and analysts in taking advantage of the opportunities of knowledge management and addressing its challenges.
ISBN: 0-7879-6291-0

IR112 **Balancing Qualitative and Quantitative Information for Effective Decision Support**
Richard D. Howard, Kenneth W. Borland Jr.
Establishes methods for integration of numeric data and its contextual application. With theoretical and practical examples, contributors explore the techniques and realities of creating, communicating, and using balanced decision support information. Chapters discuss the critical role of measurement in building institutional quality; examples of conceptual and theoretical frameworks and their application for the creation of evaluation information; and methods of communicating data and information in relation to its decision support function.
ISBN: 0-7879-5796-8

IR111 **Higher Education as Competitive Enterprise: When Markets Matter**
Robert Zemsky, Susan Shaman, Daniel B. Shapiro
Offers a comprehensive history of the development and implementation of Collegiate Results Instrument (CRI), a tool for mapping the connection between market forces and educational outcomes in higher education. Chapters detail the methods that CRI uses to help institutions to remain value centered by becoming market smart.
ISBN: 0-7879-5795-X